RICE

Edible

Series Editor: Andrew F. Smith

EDIBLE is a revolutionary series of books dedicated to food and drink that explores the rich history of cuisine. Each book reveals the global history and culture of one type of food or beverage.

Already published

Apple Erika Janik *Barbecue* Jonathan Deutsch and Megan J. Elias *Beef* Lorna Piatti-Farnell *Beer* Gavin D. Smith *Brandy* Becky Sue Epstein *Bread* William Rubel *Cake* Nicola Humble *Caviar* Nichola Fletcher *Champagne* Becky Sue Epstein *Cheese* Andrew Dalby *Chocolate* Sarah Moss and Alexander Badenoch *Cocktails* Joseph M. Carlin *Curry* Colleen Taylor Sen *Dates* Nawal Nasrallah *Eggs* Diane Toops *Figs* David C. Sutton *Game* Paula Young Lee *Gin* Lesley Jacobs Solmonson *Hamburger* Andrew F. Smith *Herbs* Gary Allen *Hot Dog* Bruce Kraig *Ice Cream* Laura B. Weiss *Lemon* Toby Sonneman *Lobster* Elisabeth Townsend *Milk* Hannah Velten *Mushroom* Cynthia D. Bertelsen *Nuts* Ken Albala *Offal* Nina Edwards *Olive* Fabrizia Lanza *Oranges* Clarissa Hyman *Pancake* Ken Albala *Pie* Janet Clarkson *Pineapple* Kaori O'Connor *Pizza* Carol Helstosky *Pork* Katharine M. Rogers *Potato* Andrew F. Smith *Rice* Renee Marton *Rum* Richard Foss *Salmon* Nicolaas Mink *Sandwich* Bee Wilson *Sauces* Maryann Tebben *Soup* Janet Clarkson *Spices* Fred Czarra *Tea* Helen Saberi *Whiskey* Kevin R. Kosar *Wine* Marc Millon

Rice

A Global History

Renee Marton

REAKTION BOOKS

For Ed, with love

Published by Reaktion Books Ltd
33 Great Sutton Street
London EC1V 0DX, UK
www.reaktionbooks.co.uk

First published 2014

Printed and bound in China
by Toppan Printing Co. Ltd

A catalogue record for this book is available
from the British Library

ISBN 978 1 78023 350 5

Contents

Introduction 7

1 Country and Culture 13

2 The Old World 29

3 The New World 45

4 The Rise of the Consumer 69

5 Art, Ritual and Symbolism 91

Recipes 113

Select Bibliography 130

Websites and Associations 134

Acknowledgements 136

Photo Acknowledgements 137

Index 139

Introduction

Without rice, even the cleverest housewife cannot cook.

Chinese proverb

It is possible to consume rice on a daily basis wherever you are in the world. In fact, two-thirds of the world's population already does this, chiefly in countries in which rice agriculture has long been established. Rice is also increasingly consumed in countries where large numbers of immigrants from rice-based countries have settled. China and southern Asia, northern India and other Asian countries from Indonesia to Myanmar to Japan, and western and central African countries: these areas are the birthplace of rice farming. In other places, rice arrived as an immigrant grain. Early on, the profit motive and the need to feed labourers (not necessarily simultaneously) were the twin drivers of rice cultivation and commerce. Human migration, whether voluntary or forced, paralleled rice migration. Both rice and people adapted to their new locations.

If you travel from New York to Guangzhou, breakfast will likely be *congee* or *juk*. This rice porridge, eaten by millions daily, is typically made from rice left over from the night before. You might also enjoy *congee* in Sacramento, California, where the descendants of Cantonese immigrants, who travelled to the

Yunnan woman spreading rice in the sun to dry, 2011.

u.s. because of the California Gold Rush of the 1850s, have remained. Rice was imported as sustenance for the 40,000 Chinese labourers in California. As an industry, however, rice agriculture in California did not begin in earnest until the late nineteenth century, with commercial rice farming accelerating in the 1920s. In 1850, when California became a state, most rice was imported from China. However, in 1950, rice agriculture in the Sacramento Valley was well established. And by 2008, 50 per cent of California-grown rice was being exported to Japan, Korea, Uzbekistan and Turkey.

It was Cantonese immigrants who opened the first Chinese restaurants in the u.s., which catered primarily to Chinese clientele. Americans slowly developed an interest in 'oriental' foods, and some Chinese cooks began working in private homes. For these Cantonese Chinese, unadorned rice accompanied almost all their meals (rice is usually served plain in countries where it is the staple starch). What we call 'fried rice' arose through the judicious use of leftovers. Today, fried rice can be ordered from menus as a dish on its own, representing an adaptation by and for non-Asians. After immigration laws were relaxed in the u.s. in 1965, Chinese diaspora immigrants from Taiwan, Hong Kong and Fujian expanded the definition of 'Chinese' in New York, San Francisco, Los Angeles and other cities. Their rice dishes came with them.

If you celebrate New Year's Day in Charleston, South Carolina, hoppin' John will likely be a part of the meal. This traditional African meal of rice and cowpeas, or black-eyed peas/beans, comes from the culinary repertoire of West Africans. It was brought to the British, Dutch, French, Spanish, Portuguese and the as yet unnamed usa (where rice became a premier crop) colonies by slaves, as well as to some Caribbean islands, Brazil, Peru, Cuba and Mexico by the workers in sugar cane, cotton, tobacco, indigo and other colonial plantations. Indians also came as indentured labourers to the West Indies, followed by the Chinese and others. Rice, imported at first for slaves and labourers, became a commercial enterprise. If you eat hoppin' John today, you are very likely to be of African or Caribbean descent, or both. And while you could be located in the southeastern u.s., the Caribbean islands or Mexico, you might equally be based in Detroit, Michigan, or Gary, Indiana.

You meet a friend for sushi and sake. Where are you? Tokyo? Perhaps, but wait: you hear Portuguese and English – it turns out you are in São Paulo or London. Sushi is almost global in its urban reach, although it is a relatively late developer in the world of global rice-based foods. And consider the California roll. This inside-out roll, sometimes made with brown rice, includes avocado, cucumber, carrots, omelette and herbs, but no raw fish. California rolls are found on the menus of elegant Japanese restaurants in Singapore and Kosher restaurants in Shanghai. In culinary schools in Tokyo chefs are even taught how to prepare them 'properly'.

While on the plane back to New York you read about famous rice-based meals in your in-flight magazine: paella, risotto, biryani and pilaf. These four rice meals are prepared at homes and in restaurants, at outdoor markets, on food trucks and at festivals; they are linked to Spain, Italy, India and Iran respectively. Recent historical research indicates that the origins of these dishes go as far back as the Moghul dynasties and Islamic traders.

Once back in New York, the Bangladeshi taxi driver at the airport offers you a snack of *jhal-muri*. This Kolkata speciality consists of puffed rice (*muri*) seasoned with lemon and coriander and mixed with peanuts, chopped onions and chilli. On one side of the New York street, South Indian street vendors sell *dosas*, crêpes stuffed with rice and lentils, on the other Pakistanis sell chicken rice, curry rice and lamb biryani.

While the colonial relationship between Britain and India ended in 1947, the culinary ties between these two countries had been evolving for more than a century, as immigrants from India came to the UK before, during and after independence. Many Brits returning from India longed for the flavours of that country's cuisine, and a few were able to satiate this appetite courtesy of the Indian wife or cook they brought back into the country with them. Indian immigrants integrated their culinary backgrounds into their new lives, and into ours. Street vendors and restaurants, and later prepared food manufacturers and supermarkets, accelerated this transmission.

You feel ill from overeating. To settle your stomach, you prepare a soothing bowl of cream of rice (remarkably similar to *congee*). You also drink *horchata*, a cooling rice-based drink from Central America and Mexico. You start a diet of puffed brown rice crackers and rice-based green tea, with an occasional

Budweiser beer; yes, rice is a principal ingredient of Budweiser. You make Rice Krispie treats for your children, and feed rice to your dog. Is rice in pet food? You guessed right. Rice is everywhere, and these examples are just the tip of the 'riceberg'. Finally, when you feel recovered, you prepare a rice pudding, studded with raisins and pistachios, to take to a dinner party for dessert.

Sticky rice scented by being cooked in bamboo.

I
Country and Culture

Whether steamed in banana leaves, simmered in pots or cooked in an electric rice cooker, rice is frequently a white canvas on which culinary cultures are painted. *Kimchi*, soy sauce, salt pork, dried fish, yams or oysters: these seasonings and/or accompaniments to rice imply heritage origins. In rice cultures, rice is testimony that you are having a meal, and is the main source of caloric energy in the diet. White, polished grains are generally the preferred form of rice but partially milled rice is also widely consumed: it is less labour-intensive to produce, costs less to procure and is more nutritious than white rice. When ground, rice can form the basis of noodles, flatbreads, cakes and crackers. Rice flour is used as a thickener for sauces, puddings, sausages, baby food and pet food, and is also used in cosmetics. Other products in which rice is a constituent include rice paper wrappers, vinegar, miso, bran oil, beer, rice 'milk' and 'wine'. Puffed, popped and flaked rice is used to make cereals, snacks, crackers, pastries and breads. Stalks and husks are woven into sandals and mats, or are burned as fuel.

How Rice Grows

Rice is a highly adaptable cereal grass that grows in most environments, but not necessarily prolifically. Irrigated rice accounts for 50 per cent of cultivated rice, and represents 75 per cent of the almost 700 million tons of rice harvested in 2010 (of which about 30 to 35 per cent is lost to husking, milling and polishing). Wetland rice begins as nursery seedlings that are later transplanted to paddies. This is an arduous and physically demanding process that produces one, two or three crops per year (depending on rice type, location and climate). Wet rice agriculture is found primarily in tropical latitudes: southern China and Southeast Asia, other Asian countries, India, Africa, the U.S., Mexico and South America. Rain-fed lowland rice accounts for another 20 per cent and upland rice for 5 per cent. Upland rice agriculture, also called dry cultivation, is found chiefly in South America and Africa. Finally, there is deep-water rice, which can grow in water depths of 50 cm (30 in) or more, and is a significant crop in Bangladesh and other areas with deeply flooded river valleys. Rice plants grow rapidly above rising water, up to 4 m (14 ft).

As the world's population increases and cities expand, rice producers strive to keep pace with demand. Along with higher yields and soil-friendly irrigation methods, vertical agriculture may provide a partial solution: essentially a variation on land-based terraced rice paddies, this approach involves growing rice in vertical layers up the sides of buildings or in giant greenhouses. Newer high-yield rice strains are being developed to accommodate increasing demand. 'Organic' rices are being explored for flavour and sustainability, while the latest news about arsenic being found in rice is being evaluated and methods for reducing it explored. While arsenic is a naturally occurring mineral that is absorbed through plant roots, the levels have been increasing recently, especially in California rice. This is being investigated at present, but so far there are no definitive causal explanations.

The Cultural and Culinary Value of Rice

White rice lends itself to multiple preparations and cultural heritages. If you ate a *puso* (rice cooked in a leaf packet), before 1965, you were probably Filipino and in Manila. After the relaxation of immigration quotas in the u.s. in 1965, you might very well have been in Daly City, California, where large numbers of immigrant Filipinos settled.

Brown rice, a complex carbohydrate with little fat, chollesterol or sodium, contains eight amino acids, B vitamins, iron, calcium and fibre. It is very nutritious and has a chewy

Liberian woman sifting rice: how to get unblemished white rice.

Bag of brown rice in burlap, ready for trade.

texture and nutty flavour. So why do most people prefer white rice? White rice stores well once the bran and germ are removed, cooks quickly and is inexpensive, digestible and satisfying. The colour white also has a long-standing symbolic value: purity, cleanliness, status and quality.

Cooked rice can be very soft, as in *congee*, or as hard as the *tahdig* (golden crust) at the bottom of a pilaf. Rice can be salty or sweet, soft or crunchy, hot or cold, and even used as a tool itself: sticky rice is especially amenable to being pressed by one's fingers into a mini bowl, which is then dragged through sauces and picks up small pieces of meat, fish or vegetables. It is endlessly versatile.

In areas with the highest rice consumption rice provides two-thirds of the daily calorie intake of the people who live there. Four more traits explain why rice has such loyal fans: first, it complements other flavours, as in pilaf or rice pudding, while maintaining its own flavour and texture. Second, rice is a buffer for spiciness, as in a vindaloo, curry or gumbo.

White rice in red bowl on black background: beautiful!

Third, rice retains moisture, enhancing succulence, as in stuffed grape leaves or boudin sausage. And finally, the inclusion of rice generally reduces meal costs.

Foremost a staple food for people living at or near subsistence levels, rice has recently become an upscale item in 'developed' countries. Statistics make clear that as people become more affluent they consume more animal protein. As discretionary income rises, high-status protein foods are sought out. Yet in industrialized countries, health concerns currently trump status displays and brown rice intake is increasing, with concomitant decreases in meat and fish. However, as the population increases, so will the need for rice, and that rice will probably be white.

According to the International Rice Research Institute (IRRI) in the Philippines, individual rice consumption by weight was highest in the following twenty countries in 2010. Rice is measured in kilograms consumed, per person, per year. China, India and Indonesia are not at the top of this list in terms of consumption per person, but are still the leading producers and consumers of rice in the world because of the size of their populations.

Rice consumed yearly per capita in kilograms

Brunei	245	Sri Lanka	97
Vietnam	166	Guinea	95
Laos	163	Sierra Leone	92
Bangladesh	160	Guinea-Bissau	85
Myanmar	157	Guyana	81
Cambodia	152	Nepal	78
Philippines	129	Korea, DPR	77
Indonesia	125	China	77
Thailand	103	Malaysia	77
Madagascar	102	Korea, Republic of	76

In comparison, annual rice intake in Brazil in 2008 was 44 kg (81 lb) per person (partially thanks to sushi consumption, particularly in São Paulo), and in the u.s., 11 kg (20¼ lb) per person.

Because Asian rice (*Oryza sativa*) is the dominant rice family from which most cultivars are descended, and as cultivars vary greatly in sensory attributes, *terroir* – the particular environment in which a plant is grown, including climate, geology and geography – is important not only for plant genetics, but for flavour, colour and aroma. There are more than 115,000 rice cultivars. Since rice agriculture is very labour-intensive and also requires vast quantities of water for maximum yields, you might wonder why people for whom rice is the daily staple would go to so much trouble to produce it. In this question lies the answer: people are loyal to the grain precisely because they have worked so hard to grow it. (This preference continues when people move to cities, but is expressed in different ways: for example, having a meal without rice in a city still means that a 'true' meal has not taken place, but perhaps a snack). And each migrational group wants its 'own' rice to be available. The fieldwork is worth it: rice yields and calories consumed are higher per acre than those for wheat, maize, soya beans and millets.

Types and Forms of Rice

Which rice do you prefer: brown, Basmati, sticky or Uncle Ben's? While we are familiar with these descriptions, they are not a real taxonomy, since rice varies in grain size, shape, colour, stickiness, taste and aroma. Remove the hull (or husk, the protective shell that covers the grains) and you are left with brown rice, which still retains the bran, germ and nutrients. Removing these elements gives you white rice, which is almost pure starch.

Types of rice: the rainbow collection.

Rice-husking machine, Yunnan, China.

Basmati is a long-grain, usually aged, usually white, aromatic Indian, Pakistani or Bangladeshi rice, highly valued for its popcorn-like aroma and ability to fluff well after cooking. The grains remain separate from one another.

Sticky rice grains can be long or short and cling together after cooking. Sticky rice may be used as a 'tool' to literally 'pick up' other parts of the meal. Some say sticky rice is more filling than other types of rice. Long-grain sticky rice is found in Thai, Laotian and southwestern Chinese communities.

Uncle Ben's is the brand name of 'converted' rice, in which nutrients from the bran covering are 'pushed' into the core during parboiling, retaining 80 per cent of the nutritional benefits. Harvested and packaged in the u.s. by Masterfoods, Inc., a subsidiary of Mars Inc., Uncle Ben's Rice is a global brand.

Indica rice grows in tropical and subtropical regions and accounts for more than 75 per cent of global trade. Indica rice cooks dry, and the grains remain separate.

Japonica rice typically grows in cooler climates and accounts for about 10 per cent of the global rice trade. Japonica grains stick together somewhat and can be eaten easily with chopsticks.

Aromatic rice, primarily Jasmine from Thailand and Basmati from India, Pakistan or Bangladesh, accounts for more than 10 per cent of global trade and typically sells at a premium in world markets. All are long-grain, with distinctive aromas, and fluff well after cooking.

Glutinous rice from Southeast Asia is used in desserts and ceremonial dishes and accounts for 5 per cent of global trade. Glutinous rice is moulded into logs and balls to be used for dipping into sauces and curries or is made into 'wrappers' for sweet or savoury fillings. There is no connection between glutinous rice and gluten, the protein found in wheat, rye and barley.

As with most attempts to classify such a diverse and adaptable cereal grass, the four categories of rice the USDA recognizes – indica, japonica, aromatic and glutinous – exclude javanica rice, which falls somewhere between the indica and japonica varieties. The USDA also omits the fact that in northern Thailand, in Laos and in Yunnan province, China, glutinous rice is not only used for sweets but is also eaten as part of the main meal. American versions of Jasmine and Basmati rice are called, among other names, Jazzmen and Texmati: while they may be similar to Jasmine and Basmati, they are not included in the classification system, although that may change through lobbying in Washington, DC.

Rice has two main starches: amylose and amylopectin. The ratio of one to the other determines the fluffiness or stickiness of cooked rice. Sticky rice has a rounder, shorter grain and very limited amounts of amylose. Once cooked, sticky rice can be moulded into a slab, or rolled into balls for dipping. Rice balls are used in the same way that a slice of baguette or wedge of naan would be in wheat-based cuisines: for picking up sauce or pieces of meat or fish. Sticky rice can be used as a 'wrapper' for vegetables, bean paste or fruit and for dumplings.

Glutinous rice is a staple food in southern China, Laos and Thailand, where rice is soaked and steamed. In Japan, Korea and northern China, somewhat less sticky rice is preferred, while medium sticky rice is most desired in Indonesia, the

Philippines, Malaysia and Vietnam. These rices are of the japonica or javanica variety and are in the mid-range of the sticky to fluffy rice continuum.

While Thailand, Vietnam and the u.s. are the top three exporters of indica rice, sticky rice fans are increasing worldwide. Sweet or *mochi* rice is another form of glutinous rice, which is favoured and grown in southwest China, Southeast Asia and Japan and used for puddings and as coverings for desserts. Glutinous and non-glutinous rice is sometimes mixed together in order to achieve specific tastes, textures and levels of malleability. When eaten plain, glutinous rice is sometimes served in the woven steamer basket in which it was cooked.

Short-grain rice is traditionally used in paella, but medium rice is often used as well. A paella pan is wide and shallow with two handles. A mixture of aromatics and/or meat is

Sticky rice cooked and served in a steamer basket: this rice is your utensil.

sautéed in the pan, dry rice is stirred in, and hot liquid is added. A classic version would contain rabbit or snails; a modern version might include shellfish, chicken or vegetables. Paella is traditionally cooked on an outdoor fire or grill and should remain uncovered during cooking, until all the liquid is absorbed. Once the liquid has been absorbed, the heat is increased and a *soccarat* forms: a layer of browned crunchy rice at the bottom of the pan. A contemporary twist involves sautéeing the aromatics and rice first; then the other ingredients and liquid are added to the pan, and it is covered and placed in the oven to finish cooking.

At the other end of the rice continuum are long-grain rices: the so-called basmatis and jasmines of the world. (True Basmati and Jasmine rices, with a capital first letter, come from India, Pakistan and Bangladesh (for Basmati) and Thailand

Finger food: glutinous rice balls with coconut and toasted sesame seeds.

Street food: Thai sticky rice in banana leaves.

(Jasmine) respectively – specific land areas that produce specific rice with protected names. When long-grain rice not of this exact type but of a similar style is referred to, however, the lower case is used: basmati and jasmine.) After cooking they elongate to two or three times their raw length. The grains remain separate after cooking. Soaked, rinsed until clear, boiled like pasta, or simmered or steamed over a very low heat in a covered pot or pan: these are the rice-cooking methods for preparing this rice plain. Dishes such pilafs and biryanis, soups and baked rice dishes, where other ingredients are added to the rice before serving, employ different cooking methods. In pilafs, for example, the rice is first sautéed in fat (originally fat from fat-tailed sheep, a prized ingredient in Persia) before being combined with a hot liquid such as stock.

Other ingredients are added to the rice at different stages of the cooking process. A pilaf with chicken, raisins and chickpeas will end up with mixing all the ingredients together simultaneously. Pouring ghee (clarified butter) down a hole in the centre of the rice, sealing the pot with a flour/water paste or a towel and letting it steam over a low heat creates a *tahdig*: a crunchy brown crust on the bottom of the pot, which is very similar to the *soccarat* in paella. Alternating layers of lamb and rice, seasoned and cooked separately and almost cooked through before they are combined in layers, gives us biryani rice dishes, of which there are multiple variations. In China, the crunchy rice crust is called *guo ba*, in Korea *nurungji* and in Senegal *xoon*.

Developments in Rice

Rice production was a beneficiary of the Green Revolution of the 1940s to 1970s, the scientific developments in agriculture that improved crop yields and disease resistance and are thought to have saved more than 1 billion people from starvation. In 1970, the Nobel Peace Prize was awarded to Norman Borlaug – the first for an agronomist – for his pioneering work in developing high-yield and semi-dwarf varieties of wheat and maize in Mexico. His methods were used later for growing rice and wheat in Asia, through the auspices of the International Rice Research Institute (IRRI), which has a repository of thousands of rice species, as well as funding ongoing research projects to increase the yield of rice plants while reducing pests and plant disease outbreaks. The IRRI developed varieties of high-yielding rice seeds. This work continues today with research into rice with higher yields and lower water requirements. Korea became self-sufficient in rice production after switching to high-yield rice varieties and modern management methods. India has begun to use laser levelling – using lasers to flatten the land and create rows – for rice fields. This is less arduous than physically levelling the land, and the resultant fields use less water during irrigation.

Rice paddy irrigation results in the production of methane gas, a contributor – albeit a small one – to global warming. Land used for biofuel production (instead of harvesting plants for human consumption) and genetically engineered (GE) rice: these controversial topics remain tied to the future of rice. Some countries have returned to traditional rice agriculture, even as they are using modern seeds (Indonesia, since the 1970s). Despite record harvests in the last ten years, coastal areas, many of which are in rice-producing areas, have already been inundated as a result of climate change.

Protecting, preserving and planting older breeds of rice is one way of avoiding future monocultures that might be susceptible to particular environmental problems or disease. The IRRI maintains a gene bank of rice cultivars as an attempt to safeguard against the practice of monocultures.

Other scientific developments in rice may solve other potential problems. The Central Rice Research Institute in Cuttack, India, in 2010 developed a rice variety with very low amylose: aghonibora. The advantage of lower starch levels is that less water is needed to produce ready-to-eat rice. It has only to be soaked in warm water for 30 minutes before it is ready to consume. Floodplain rice is also being looked into as an alternative grain for the future, since climate change may lead to flooding in many parts of the world. The Cuu Long Delta Rice Research Institute in Vietnam was established to develop high-yield rice strains with a short planting season and the ability to be planted away from the Mekong Delta floodplain, which is expected to disappear as sea levels rise. In the U.S., the Rice Research and Extension Center Institute in Stuttgart, Arkansas (Arkansas produces 50 per cent of U.S. rice), maintains efforts to keep American rice competitive in the global market, and to research newer varieties for the future.

Through the research and development of sustainable ways of farming, rice will remain available to those who already depend on it for daily sustenance, as well as for the population of the future.

2

The Old World

Approximately 15,000 years ago, the ability to domesticate plants turned some hunter-gatherers into agrarian communities. Certain cereals were preferred: wheat, barley, millets, sorghum and rice. Some historians suggest that women were the first rice cultivators because they were also the main gatherers. They fished at the river's edge, where rice grew. Other historians maintain that rice began as an upland crop. Nature, climate, human usage and migration directed rice's move towards water.

Rice was farmed like other plants, in a forest clearing. Shifting cultivation – called swidden, or slash-and-burn, agriculture – is still used in some upland areas of Southeast Asia and western Africa. Higher yields were obtained through controlled irrigation. Yield intensification produced many innovations, including 'puddling', which creates a belowground level of flat, hard earth. This prevents water from draining away quickly, and breaks down the internal soil structure. Young rice plants gain a foothold over weeds. This method extended use of a limited water supply. Nursery seedlings are transplanted to standing water after one to six weeks. Puddling was probably developed in India, refined and expanded in China, and is used all over the world today.

Rice panicle – each grain of rice is visible.

Other cultivars evolved in the warm, wet and humid areas of southern Asia and the subcontinent, and adapted to differing terrains: lowland rice evolved near rivers and estuaries; upland rice grew on flatlands and mountain slopes in drier and colder climes. In floodplains, rice varieties evolved that could withstand rising waters, with the rice panicle (branching flower clusters with rice grains) remaining above the water.

China, Mostly

The history of rice begins in the foothills of the Himalayas in northeastern India, in Southeast Asia, southern China and Indonesia. Domestication evolved in India and China and subsequently arrived in Korea, Japan, the Philippines, Sri Lanka and Indonesia. Archaeologists have discovered carbonized rice grains pressed into pottery shards in the southern Yangtzi River Valley in China, in Spirit Cave in Thailand, in Koldihwa in Uttar Pradesh, India, and in Sorori, Korea.

Fossilized beetles that ate stored rice near carbonized rice grains were also found. The earliest grains, to date, were growing some 15,000 years ago. And glutinous rice, cooked into a thick porridge and mixed with lime and sand, was used as mortar for the 10-kg (22-lb) bricks that make up the Great Wall of China.

Boiling and/or steaming rice is the fastest, easiest way to make it edible. If the grains are soaked first, they get a head start in absorption and remain supple so they don't break when being stirred during cooking. However, if you have many broken grains, you make porridge. Or, if you pound the grains in a pestle and mortar (which you also do to remove the bran covering), you can make flat breads or noodles. Rice paper was a food 'wrapper', especially in Southeast Asia and southwest China. (These wrappers should not be confused with the rice

Nepalese rice sickle, with a blade cover, so the gods won't notice when you cut the plant.

Rice noodles.

paper that is used by painters or employed for other non-edible functions: edible rice paper wrappers are made from rice flour and water; sometimes egg is added to create dough; non-edible rice paper is made from the straw left on the rice plant after harvesting.) Rice stalks became baskets, mats and sandals, or were burned as fuel. Husks and rice bran oil were used as animal feed, although today rice bran oil is found at upscale supermarkets for cooking and salad dressings.

Beginning in the sixth century CE, southern China became the rice granary for the country; northern China was the political centre, concerned with guarding the border and maintaining hegemony. Rice fed soldiers and prevented famines. *Congee*, a boiled rice porridge or gruel, was then and is still a common meal, even in the north, where wheat and millet were eaten extensively. Called *juk* in Korea, *kanji* in India and *okayu* in Japan, *congee* is found all over the world. One thousand years later, we have Italian risotto and American Cream of Rice cereal: not so different from congee... and yet, both of these soupy rice preparations are unlike congee because of the specific rice and cooking methods used, the function of rice at the meal and consumer demographics. One might say that rice puddings are congees that have been sweetened and stiffened.

During the Song Dynasty (960–1279 CE), Champa rice from present-day Vietnam came to southern China. This rapid-ripening and drought-resistant rice quickly became dominant because it was possible to yield two or three crops each planting season. 'Rice men', specialist rice farmers called *nongshi*, were encouraged to innovate, both in cultivation methods and technology. These men were literate and implemented government policy as they went from village to village. Champa rice provided reliable rice supplies for the farmer, and the second crop was his – after he paid the landlord and taxes – along with the first. The government supported knowledge of rice varieties that could withstand differences in climate, altitude and soil, as well as provide high yields. Rice farmers were skilled in the particular rice cultivars whose seeds they saved, planted, harvested, ate, stored or traded. Hybrids of rice varietals were common, as farmers saved seeds that

Back-breaking work: rice paddy workers.

provided rice plants with desirable characteristics. As a result, rice agriculture became dominant and varied, and when more land was needed, people moved to look for more exploitable terrain. When Marco Polo travelled to China from 1271 to 1295 CE after the Mongolian conquest, he was served rice wine at the palace of the Kublai Khan at Cathay.

For the tables of the Chinese Emperor and his Court, however, white rice was a luxury product. According to one account, a period of culinary excellence occurred during the Mongolian reign of Emperor Qianlong (1736–1796). Court banquets included soups, fish, meat, vegetables, noodles and sweets. White rice might be served to accompany some dishes, but often it was part of the recipe: lotus root stuffed with glutinous rice, or rice powder dumplings. A rice porridge called *chou* was taken after meals, presumably to aid digestion, since rice porridge was a standard treatment for stomach upset (which is still recommended today) and overeating at banquets was the norm. A seasonal example of *chou* is the La Pa ('harvest') Festival porridge with fruits, nuts and beans.

Water-filled Yunnan rice terraces before planting season.

In 2010, world rice production provided 20 per cent of all calories consumed. One-third was contributed by China, which also fed 25 per cent of the world's population from just 7 per cent of its arable land. Since only between 5 and 10 per cent of the rice produced in the world is traded at all – most is consumed locally – any fluctuations in price, due to climate or politics, has a disproportionate influence on rice in the global market. As urbanization continues, skilled rice farmers are moving to cities, and while mechanization is having some influence on present-day rice agriculture, the loss of skilled rice farmers is worrisome.

Trade and Asia

Within and outside China, rice travelled on barges along canals. The Grand Canal, which was 1,776 km (1,103 m) long and transported goods from Hangzhou in the south to Beijing in the north, brought rice to the military. Rice also moved along various 'silk' roads, via donkey and camel caravans. The famous Silk Road, which we are accustomed to hearing about, ran from Central Asia to the Persian Gulf and Mediterranean coasts. The Southwest Silk Road began in Sichuan Province and crossed present-day India (first known as Bharat and later as Hindustan) ending in Bactria, a central Asian kingdom. And finally the Maritime Silk Road led to several ports: Jiaozhou (present-day North Vietnam) and Guangzhou. The Maritime Silk Road wrapped around Indochinese coasts through the straits of Malacca, ending in the Indian Ocean and Persian Gulf.

Of course, ships carried a lot more weight than camels, especially when luxury goods such as spices, furs, ceramics and textiles were being transported. Each transport method had advantages and drawbacks, so all were used. Animals must be fed and maintained, and may become ill. Barges are very slow. Sailing ships rely on prevailing winds ('trade' winds), and often sink, whether from storms or pirate attacks.

Rice was traded for tin (important as an alloy ingredient, as well as a coating for more toxic metals), almonds, wood, ceramics, cowries, ivory, incense and spices. Rice was also used as currency. Certain weights in rice were used as evaluative measures for barter, even when the rice itself did not change hands. It was the gold standard of its time. Rice was also used as ballast on sailing ships, and then sold when the ships arrived in port. Aged rice was considered tastier than fresh rice, so it had an edge over competing grains like wheat, which travelled less hardily.

Ports and islands were hubs or entrepôts where rice was traded. The accompanying map shows how often rice was traded in the Malaysian entrepôt of Malacca.

Arab or Indian traders (Muslims) are thought to have brought rice noodles to Indonesia and the Malay Peninsula as early as the thirteenth century CE. Buddhism, Hinduism and Islam influenced rice cookery. Rice was the basis of most meals, and accompanied the meats, fish and vegetables that were and still are served as curries with *sambals*, spicy condiments made with shrimp paste and tamarind juice. Javanica rice (from Java) is used for curries, while desserts use glutinous rice.

In the 1600s, China set up trading centres on the western coast of Malaysia, and Chinese migrants went to Indonesia. Warehouses and docking facilities had been established in the Strait of Malacca centuries earlier. These narrow protected waters allowed Chinese, Indian and Arabian Gulf ships to meet and trade. The men who travelled to these coasts often married the Malay and Indonesian women they met there. Known as *nonyas*, an honorary title, Malay wives blended their own culinary backgrounds with those of the Chinese. Chinese

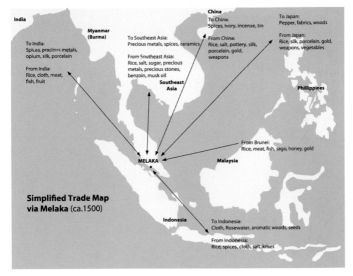

Malacca map: rice has been traded for millennia, and still is today.

recipes, wok cooking, spices and ingredients from the Malay community fused into a melting-pot cuisine. Malaysian cookery continues to link four heritages: Malay, Chinese, Indian and Nyonya. Hot chillies and *umami*-rich condiments such as fermented shrimp paste offset the mildness of rice and the richness of coconut milk. Since Muslims are the majority population in Malaysia and do not eat pork, while the Chinese do, and Hindus do not eat beef, they are all linked by their love of rice. In *ikan briani*, a layered rice and spiced fish dish, one suspects the influence of Moghuls from Afghanistan and northern India in the biryani layering technique. Fish fillets seasoned with onions, garlic, ginger, coriander and cumin alternate with layers of spiced long-grain rice seasoned with ghee, cardamom, cloves and cinnamon, the whole finished with chopped ripe tomatoes and thick coconut milk: whether you were Hindu, Buddhist or Muslim, you could eat this meal.

Other dishes were served with unadorned steamed rice, with a spiced accompaniment, such as a fish curry or vinegared chicken. As the Sumatran cookery and foodways writer Sri Owen has noted, rice-focused countries tend to serve rice plain, with everything else on the side.

Another example of *nonya* cooking is the dessert *pulut hitam*, made with glutinous black rice, jaggery, pandan leaves and coconut milk: served with sliced ripe bananas and thick coconut milk, its resemblance to rice pudding is clear, even if the rice is sticky and does not require eggs to bind it, and the jaggery, pandan leaves and coconut milk are replaced in the American/European cupboard by white rice, white sugar and dairy milk, whether fresh or condensed. Instead of ripe bananas and coconut milk, an American version could be made with raisins, while a French version might include candied fruits and nuts, and an Italian version, glazed chestnuts.

A popular Malaysian breakfast is *lakhsha*, a fiery blend of rice noodles mixed with chilli-infused coconut milk, dried

Malaysian rice pudding with coconut milk and toasted cashews.

shrimp paste, chicken, lemongrass and coriander. The word *lakhsha* comes from the Persian word for noodle. Persians introduced noodle-making to China during the Han Dynasty (206 BCE –220 CE), so it is thought.

Indian Influence

Rice may have been domesticated independently in Afghanistan and northern India at least 5,000 years ago. It spread west to the Indus Valley and south into peninsular India. Rice cultivation began near the Ganges around 2500 BCE. Semi-nomadic hunters and fishermen moved regularly to avoid Mongol invaders from Central Asia, and to find arable land. Around 2000 BCE, these Indo-Aryans moved into the Caucasus, Persia and the Hindu Kush Mountains, settling in Punjab, Delhi and Afghanistan. The five rivers of the Punjab irrigate much of the rice grown in India, even though rice consumption in southern India is greater than in the north. From the Moghal influence comes *pilaus* with cream, fruit and nuts in meat and rice preparation. *Idlis* and *dosas* – both fermented products (souring and fermentation lowered bacterial contamination risk and extended 'shelf life') – and rice and dal (lentils) are more common as you head south. For Kashmiris, pilaf is seasoned with cumin, cloves, cinnamon and cardamom. For Bengalis, the 'holy trinity' flavour profile includes fish, rice and mustard seed oil, just as celery, green onions and green peppers are the 'holy trinity' of Cajun cookery, and *mirepoix* (carrots, celery and onions) for French cookery. For Keralans, curry leaves and coconut perfume rice. Mutton curry with rice showcases the Muslim influence.

When Europeans began colonizing Asia in the late Middle Ages, rice was known as 'batty' in southern India and as 'paddy' in the north. Both terms come from Sanskrit 'Bhakta', which refers to boiled rice. Families farmed small plots of land, producing high yields. In a good year, if the rice deities were pleased and smiled favourably on the family (or if the land owner was pleased with his rice payments), enough rice was produced to provide for the family's immediate needs, with excess rice stored or traded.

Rice can be stored as seed (still in the husk) or as white rice, but not easily in between. The bran and the germ/embryo each contain fat, which quickly becomes rancid in tropical climates. Removing the bran layer and the germ, using a pestle and mortar, results in whitish rice. There are multiple bran layers, so some bran will normally remain unless the rice is completely polished, at which point it becomes white rice and can be stored for years. For some, rice that has been stored for a long time has improved flavour and cooking ability: the grains fluff better after cooking because they have dried out more.

Indica rice is thought to have moved from the Indian subcontinent and Southeast Asia into Sri Lanka, Malaysia, Indonesia and China south of the Yangtze River. Javanica rice became the upland rice of Southeast Asia and the lowland rice of Indonesia, from which it spread to the Philippines, Taiwan and Japan.

India also produces flaked and puffed rice, used in snacks, breakfast and religious ceremonies. Flaked rice can be eaten raw or with milk and sugar (this sounds similar to Rice Krispies, although that rice *is* puffed). Puffed rice is often found in *chaat*, a snack with many variations. *Bhel puri*, a popular street snack in India and in the Indian diaspora, includes puffed rice, potatoes, tomatoes, mint chutney, crunchy gram-flour threads, peanuts, lemon juice, chillies and coriander. A total of 10 per cent of all Indian rice production is utilized for flaked, expanded and popped rice.

Islamic Influence

As early as 1000 BCE, rice spread to the Middle East from India via Afghanistan and Persia. Around 500 BCE, the Persian Empire under the Achmaenids incorporated Asia as far as the Indus River, including Greece, North Africa, Egypt and Libya. Persian influence moved to India via Iran and Afghanistan, spread by Muslim Arab traders, who travelled on to North Africa, Turkey and Greece, arriving in Italian ports, especially Venice and, later, Spain.

Invading Moors from northwestern Africa colonized Southern Europe and brought rice to Sicily, Southern Spain and North Africa in the tenth century. By the mid-1400s, commercial rice production had begun in northern Italy. Islamic gastronomy was centred in the Abbasid capital of Baghdad, then a cultural and culinary melting pot for the Islamic world, whose agriculture, ingredients and foodways travelled to Spain. The Spanish city of Cordoba became an Islamic cultural and gastronomic capital. Olives, limes, capers, aubergine and rose petals, as well as apricots, artichokes, carob, saffron, sugar, jujube, citrus fruits and carrots, were used in cookery. A condiment similar to fish sauce was made from barley (*murri*) or fish. Long-grain rice was used to make pilaus of all kinds (*pilaf, pilau* and *pulao* are variations of the same word); the paellas, which use short- or medium-grain rice, might be seen as distant cousins. Rice was stuffed into fruits, vegetables, vine leaves and sausages.

Alexander the Great brought rice to Greece from India in the early fourth century BCE. An expensive luxury product, rice was used primarily for medicinal purposes but was also found occasionally at banquets. The Greek physicians Galen and Anthimus both recommended rice gruel with goat's milk for stomach problems, and the rice had to be well cooked.

Rice being boiled for a Persian Sultan, from the Ni'matnama-i Nasir al-Din Shah (*c.* 1500).

Here is a prescription for an upset stomach from Anthimus:

> Boil rice in fresh water. When it is properly cooked, strain off the water and add goat's milk. Put the pot on the flame and cook slowly until it becomes a solid mass. It is eaten like this, but not cold, but without salt and oil.

In the seventh century CE, Muslim traders brought Asiatic rice to the Mediterranean. While Muslim Arabs had been trading with China and smaller Asian nations for centuries, they expanded their horizons by turning their focus to Mediterranean cultures and adapted their agricultural methods to Spain, Sicily and Italy, Egypt and Syria. In Egypt, rice was planted near the Nile: the irrigation and transport benefits of the river made Egypt a transport hub for the rice trade. The water-wheel system, known in Roman, Persian, Chinese and Arabian agriculture systems, promoted rice agriculture in the Valencia region of Spain, in Sicily and eventually in the Pô Valley in northern Italy. First built by Romans, norias were giant water wheels. Buckets attached to the wheels' rims deposited water into large and small irrigation canals. More than 8,000 norias were built in Spain. The remains of these water wheels can still be found throughout Spain today.

Spanish noria: ancient water wheel that still exists today.

Madagascar rice pot: aluminum pot over outdoor hearth.

3
The New World

African rice (*Oryza glaberrima*) had been cultivated for thousands of years, primarily in West African coastal countries, in Central Africa and in Madagascar. Red in colour, this rice originates from the Niger River delta, and is the other leading rice family after *O. sativa*, Asian rice. This African staple has significant characteristics distinguishing it from Asian rice. It should be noted that, until the late twentieth century, African rice had not been a major object of academic study. Carl Linnaeus did not include it in his botanical classifications. And wilful ignorance of the importance of African agriculture also accounts for delays in researching its history. In the last 30 years, renewed interest has generated much new research and information on African rice. A comparison of the two plants is helpful.

African rice is somewhat salt-tolerant, a useful trait for irrigation near seawater. The grain is dark red and smaller and nuttier in flavour than Asian rice. It grows vertically without drooping, and is more easily harvested than its Asian counterpart, which is top-heavy when ripe. However, in a pestle and mortar, African grains shatter more easily than Asian grains; finesse, skill and practice are needed to obtain unbroken grains. Along with sorghum, millets, yams, okra and other plants, African rice was a staple plant.

Both rice and slaves were taken to the colonies of the British, Portuguese, French and Spanish empires. Africans from the 'Rice Coast' countries of West Africa, including Gambia, Angola, Guinea, Guinea-Bissau, Sierra Leone and southern Senegal, as well as the Niger River delta, were sought after for their rice-agriculture expertise. A rice trade triangle developed between Great Britain, West Africa and Western Europe.

Once African rice was planted in the New World, it became critical in the early development of the colonial rice industry, although there was an eventual switch from African to Asian rice for commerce. The African influence on New World 'riziculture' and culinary evolution was extensive. Both Asian and African rice have their advantages and drawbacks in the field, in the milling process and in the kitchen. In the late twentieth century, a hybrid of both kinds of rice, called NERICA (New Rice for Africa), was developed, and has shown promise for the future of African rice. Not only can this rice be grown on upland terrains, it is more pest-resistant and has higher yields than traditional rice, as well as a shorter maturation time: 90–100 days as opposed to 120–40 days.

Liberian feast ladle, early 20th century: scoop the rice grains while honouring our animal ancestors.

The British Colonies and South Carolina

British traders who owned sugar plantations in Barbados, Jamaica and the West Indies discovered that South Carolina's rivers, streams, marshes, tidal basins and subtropical climate were ideal for rice growing. Demand in Europe for high-quality long-grain rice was high. Traders knew that rice would be profitable.

Around 1685, it is said, the physician and botanist Dr Henry Woodward received a packet of seed rice from a ship's captain, temporarily marooned in Charleston. This was *O. glaberrima*, African red rice. Other stories maintain that women and child slaves working in the colonies smuggled in unhusked rice in their hair. Thomas Jefferson even brought Italian rice into the area, as he explained in a letter to the politician Edward Rutledge in 1787:

> I determined to take enough [rice] to put you in seed: they informed me however its exportation in the husk was prohibited; so I could only bring off as much as my coat and surtout pockets would hold.

British plantation owners knew that the Jola, Yoruba, Igbo and Mande peoples were renowned for their rice-agriculture skills, from planting seedlings to building canals and dykes. The Portuguese acknowledged their skills as early as the mid-1400s. These Africans received the highest bids at slave auctions. From inserting a rice seed into a moist clod of earth that would not float away during irrigation, to hoeing, transplanting seedlings, weeding, harvesting, pounding, and husking, slaves worked in the fields, creating 'factories in the field', or rather the colonial rice plantations of South Carolina. African slaves were so adept at every part of rice agriculture that the plantation ran as smoothly as a modern factory, and with an equally huge output. Some slaves grew their own rice (despite laws dating from 1714 making it illegal for workers to grow rice for themselves), vegetables and legumes. Some raised chickens and pigs, and foraged, fished and hunted. They added Native American ingredients to the pantry, especially corn and chillies. And they received rations from their owners, including small monthly allotments of salt, sugar and the least favoured parts of pigs.

Unfortunately, African rice grains broke easily in a pestle and mortar, thereby reducing the yield. In addition, male slaves were often required to undertake this work because female slaves, who were more skilled at milling, were often assigned to domestic chores instead.

South Carolina rice was known as 'Carolina Golde' after the golden fields of grain. It had a very high status among other forms of long-grain rice, and the white grains in particular were very expensive and won awards at European agricultural fairs. The grain was also mentioned by name in British cookbooks used in colonial kitchens.

The first American published cookbook that mentions rice is *The Compleat Housewife* by Eliza Smith (1742). The most popular British cookery book of the eighteenth century, *The Art of Cookery, Made Plain and Easy* by Hannah Glasse (1747), was very influential in colonial households. Recipes for puddings, pilaf, soup, curry and pancakes, all using rice, were included. A recipe for the rice dish hoppin' John appears in *The Carolina Housewife*, in 1847, by Sarah Rutledge, a prominent socialite. By including hoppin' John in her cookbook, Rutledge paved the way for cooking by slaves to develop into 'Southern Cooking'. Still, rice was too complex a topic to easily discuss, as this quote from Mrs Beeton's *Book of Household Management*, published in 1861, makes clear:

Varieties of Rice. – Of the varieties of rice brought to our market, that from Bengal is chiefly of the species denominated cargo rice, and is of a coarse reddish-brown cast, but peculiarly sweet and large-grained; it does not readily separate from the husk, but it is preferred by the natives to all others. Patna rice is more esteemed in Europe, and is of very superior quality; it is small-grained, rather long and wiry, and is remarkably white. The Carolina rice is considered as the best, and is likewise the dearest in London.

The following recipe from J. M. Sanderson's *The Complete Cook,* published in 1864, shows the early influence of French and British cuisine on the use of rice in cooking, and may possibly have come from a Middle Ages 'receipt' known as 'blanc manger'. This was likely derived from an Arab dish of almonds pounded into 'milk', and rice or rice flour and sugar, enhanced with shredded chicken and rosewater. This pudding has many variants in cooking, and in nomenclature.

Rice Custard. – Take a cup of whole Carolina rice, and seven cups of milk; boil it, by placing the pan in water, which must never be allowed to go off the boil until it thickens; then sweeten it, and add an ounce of sweet almonds pounded.

Some female slaves were assigned to 'the big house' kitchens. The 'mistresses' read recipes aloud from British cookbooks, expecting their cooks to prepare recipes by memorizing ingredients and methods. Despite the European origins of these recipes, African ingredients and cooking techniques (frying, for example) influenced the resulting preparations. Yams, aubergine (eggplant), okra, black-eyed beans (peas), millet,

Rice cake recipe, from Mrs Beeton.

greens, watermelon, squash, sesame seeds, sweet potatoes, kola nuts and sorghum all have an African pedigree.

While choice parts of the pig were reserved for plantation owners and their families, slaves used the hocks, heads, offal, ribs, salt pork, bacon and chitterlings as seasonings or accompaniments to meals, many of which had rice as the centrepiece. Today, these ingredients and recipes remain integral to southern American foodways, not only in black households, but some white ones as well. Rice cakes with honey were occasionally prepared, a Muslim tradition hidden from plantation owners. Senegalese and Nigerian slaves, usually Muslim, cooked their version of hoppin' John with jerked beef because of the prohibition on eating pork.

Descendants of slaves from the coastal lowlands and Sea Islands of South Carolina and Georgia, called Gullahs or Geechees, used rice to underpin all of their meals. The word Gullah refers to 'the people who eat rice for dinner'. Oysters, shrimp, fish, pork and poultry were occasional accompaniments to white rice. Rice and greens, and rice and okra, similar to

Sierra Leone's *plasas* and rice and okra soup, were more common. Red rice, when served with a gumbo (from the Bantu word *nkombo* for 'okra') containing okra, fish, tomatoes and hot peppers, resembles West African jollof rice, which has been described as a 'typical South Carolina meal' and is still typical of Gullah foodways.

By 1690, rice was a substantial commercial crop in the colonies. The speed at which the industry grew is a distinctive feature of Carolina rice culture. In 1700, 600,000 pounds of rice left Charleston harbour for Britain and the West Indies. By 1710, 1.5 million pounds of rice was being exported and by 1740, 43 million pounds. The volume was so great that rice ships became targets for pirates, who ransacked and sank them as they crossed the Atlantic. Rice exports became safer and larger after protective British warships appeared. In 1771, approximately 60 million pounds of rice was channelled through England, which collected duties, to the rest of Europe. Exports reached 80 million pounds by 1789. Fortunes

Charleston slave auction broadside, *c.* 1780s.

were made. The chart below shows rice price increases from 1772 to 1809.

Rice prices in the USA, 1772–1809

Time Period	Rice Price (cent/lb)
1722–9	1.40
1730–39	1.64
1740–49	1.18
1750–59	1.56
1760–69	1.58
1770–79	1.87
1780–89	3.15
1790–99	2.73
1800–1809	3.81

In 1750, McKewn Johnstone, a South Carolina planter, developed a way to use ocean tides to flood rice fields: this increased available land. And in 1767, Jonathan Lucas invented a water-powered mill, reducing labour requirements and producing more whole grains.

During the Civil War (1861–5), plantations were decimated. The rice industry had already begun a westward move to the prairies of Arkansas, Louisiana and Texas because flat land and machinery (rather than human labour) lowered production costs. In the meantime, chitterlings ('chitlins'), collard greens, ham hocks, grits, black-eyed peas and rice travelled with the escaped and freed slaves as they moved on to northern cities. African American populations grew in Detroit, Chicago, New York and in other cities. In 1964, the term 'soul food' was used for the first time in print to describe these subsistence food ingredients and preparations that were eaten in a spirit of ethnic pride and 'soulfulness'.

African American workers on Cape Fear River rice plantation, North Carolina, 1866, wood engraving. While most slaves were free to go, some stayed on as hired employees after the Civil War ended.

Although rice cultivation continued in South Carolina for 80 years, production was minimal, and ceased around 1920. In 2000, Anson Mills harvested its first crop of heirloom rice, and is now growing other heirloom rices. The Carolina Gold Rice Foundation in Charleston, South Carolina, announced the arrival of aromatic long-grain rice in February 2011. Both Carolina Gold and Charleston Gold are now grown.

Louisiana, the Prairie and California

As the French and Spanish vied for control of the Louisiana territories, rice cookery evolved. The words 'Creole' and 'Cajun' refer to people, ingredients and foodways resulting from European, Caribbean and African cultural and culinary mixing. Creoles began as children born to Spanish parents in Spain's older colonies. Children of French settlers and slaves born in Louisiana were added to this definition. Cajuns were French colonists evicted from Acadia in 1755 when the British gained control of Canada. Acadians ('Cajuns') drifted south and many landed in the bayous of New Orleans. Creole cookery is usually linked with wealthier New Orleans, while Cajun cookery became known a bit later, as the bayous were harder to reach, the people poorer and the food often spicier.

Gumbos are Cajun and Creole rice preparations where the rice serves different purposes. Each recipe may be either Creole or Cajun in origin, depending on whom you talk to. Feelings about gumbo's origins and proper ingredients are fierce. In Creole gumbo, you'll likely find shrimp, sausage and chicken, with rice moderating the spicy flavours and stretching the economic value of the meal. In Cajun gumbo, crawfish, crabs, possibly squirrel, andouille sausage and hot pepper might accompany the rice. Gumbo is a dish in which all the flavours are 'married' to one other; it is remarkably similar to a pilaf or paella, although is much soupier in consistency.

Another iconic Louisianan dish is 'red beans and rice'; a modification of hoppin' John that has just as many variations. Regional differences abound: annatto is added in Jamaica and coconut milk in the Dominican Republic. Hoppin' John is traditionally eaten on New Year's Day, red beans and rice on laundry day. Beans simmered with a ham hock were eaten with white rice. Greens were traditional accompaniments, with the

Crawfish gumbo: notice the rice in the lower left corner!

'pot likker' (the ambrosial water at the bottom of the greens pot) drunk as well.

When Italians, Germans and Yugoslavs immigrated to Louisiana, they added their own touches to the Creole/Cajun melting pot. Italians from Northern Italy had been immigrating to Louisiana since the time of the Spanish explorer Hernándo de Soto (c. 1496–1542), and Germans had come to New Orleans since its founding in 1718. Many Germans moved north to flatter land to become wheat, and later, rice farmers. The German influence is evident in a salad that uses the same seasonings as a German hot potato salad, with a couple of New World additions: bacon, sugar, cider vinegar, celery seed, chopped pimientos, green pepper and onion, all tossed with hot cooked rice, with a sliced hard-boiled egg on top. Boudin blanc reflects the combination of tradition with new ingredients: a sausage of ground pork, rice and spices, it combines the adaptation of German sausage-making traditions with Louisiana's agricultural products, thrift and taste preferences.

Rice and beans: upscale hoppin' John.

In the late 1800s, a farmer planted three acres of rice in Arkansas. The land was flat and could support retooled heavy machinery (originally used for wheat). Improvements in milling and irrigation methods quickly followed. Arkansas became the 'rice basket' of the U.S., as noted in the state anthem: 'There the rice fields are full.' Settlers in covered wagons brought rice to Texas and Missouri, while the Louisiana Western Railroad linking Orange, Texas, to Lafayette, Louisiana, in 1881, brought Midwestern wheat farmers to the prairies of Louisiana, Arkansas and Texas. In just 30 years (from 1880 to 1910) this virgin land, which a government assessor had declared to be of no agricultural value, became the most prolific rice area in the nation.

Midwesterners had to learn how to make fluffy rice. The Southern Rice Growers Association published educational pamphlets with recipes. In 1921, the Creole Mammy Rice Recipe booklet had recipes for gumbo, jambalaya and rice custard. Also, the nutritional value of rice was emphasized to potato-loving Germans, Czechs and Scandinavians. 'Rice and legumes' were better for you than 'wheat and meat'.

Contemporary American rice production is centred in Arkansas, California, Louisiana, Mississippi, Missouri and Texas. Most rice is long-grain, with Arkansas the leader in tonnage. Production has grown by 60 per cent in the last 30 years, on the same land. In 2010, U.S. rice production was 83 million kg (184 million lb) of long-grain, 26 million kg (57 million lb) of medium-grain and just under 1.5 million kg (3 million lb) of short-grain rice.

Farmers near Sacramento found that rice would grow better than other crops. By 1920, California was expanding into serious commercial rice production; modern 'riziculture' methods include planes spraying seeds, pesticides and fertilizers directly into the furrows of laser-levelled fields. Some 90 per cent of California rice is medium-grain, often referred to as 'Calrose'. It is used for everything from sushi to paella to Asian recipes. It has a clean, mild taste, and sticks together very slightly. In addition to Calrose, other kinds of rice are planted or imported, from organically grown short- and long-grain rices to older breeds like black 'forbidden rice', bamboo green rice and Bhutanese red rice. Organic rice farms have also become an important part of the California rice industry.

In 1919, 1 million acres were used for rice production; the yield was approximately 1,100 lbs per acre. In 2010, 3 million acres were used; the highest yields were 6,500 lbs per acre. In 1970, the rice crop was valued at $0.5 billion, and in 2010, $3 billion. Rice production is divided equally between home consumption and export.

Cuban woman
and rice painting:
contemporary art
in Havana by Nadia
García Porras, 2010.

Spain, Peru and Cuba

Between 1849 and 1874, 100,000 Chinese hired labourers,
known as 'coolies', came to the Spanish colonies based in
Cuba and Peru under eight-year contracts. Most worked on
plantations, on coastal farms or as domestics. When Peru and
Cuba became independent in the mid-1850s, slavery was
illegal and Chinese coolies had replaced slaves as indentured
labourers. They demanded rice as part of their payment. Asian
rice was imported at first, and later planted along coastal
waterways. In the 1870s, escaped and freed coolies moved into
the Peruvian Amazon, where they introduced rice, beans and
other crops. In the mid-twentieth century, Chinese Peruvians
congregated around the central market square in Lima that
became known as *el barrio chino* (Chinatown). Today, Chinese
restaurants, *chifas*, are evidence of the Chinese–Peruvian mix.

The first Chinese arrived in Cuba in 1857 and worked with
African slaves and the indigenous people. Marriages between
Chinese and Africans occurred (marriage to Spaniards was

prohibited). A total of 125,000 'coolies' eventually came to Cuba. African and Chinese rice cookery combined, resulting in some fusion dishes, while Cuban-Chinese cooking emerged from what became one of the largest groupings of Chinese in Latin America: *el barrio chino. Congee*, the southern Chinese breakfast staple, and *moros y christianos* – black beans and rice (derisively known as 'Moors and Christians') – were both eaten in Havana. After the Cuban revolution in 1959, most Chinese left for Miami and New York, where Cuban-Chinese food abounds.

Mexico

In the 1520s, Spanish conquerors introduced rice to Veracruz, Mexico. Proximity to the Gulf of Mexico made it an excellent choice for rice agriculture. In Campeche two rice crops per season were possible. Rice was introduced into the daily diet, replacing saffron with tomatoes, often cooking rice first in fat and then adding hot liquid and other ingredients.

Arroz con Pollo.

Cooking rice in fat first proved important to maintaining grain separation after cooking, because the rice was medium-grain, which tends to be somewhat sticky. The Arab/Spanish technique of cooking rice first in fat and then adding hot liquid moved to the colonies in tandem with the advance of colonial powers. Both long- and short-grain rice were planted. Asian rice came via the Pacific route, African rice via the Spanish. Asian rice eventually reigned, becoming the most frequently grown of the two grains.

The traditional duo of rice and beans did not advance into its current iconic state very rapidly. According to Rick Bayless (chef and historian of Mexican cookery and foodways) rice was adopted more fully once it was incorporated into meals that were already traditional. Usually made with medium- or long-grain rice, *sopa seca* refers to dry rice preparations where all the cooking liquid is absorbed, as in rice and seafood

Horchata: cool and refreshing; just what you need on a hot day.

preparations from Veracruz. *Sopas aguadas*, literally 'wet soups', are a stew or thick soup. For the sweet-toothed there is *arroz con leche*, Mexican rice pudding. And for cool relief from the heat, *horchata*, a chilled beverage made of soaked ground rice that is strained and flavoured with almonds or cinnamon.

Portugal and Brazil

Rice cultivation came to Bahia, on the east coast of Brazil, in 1530 when a Dutch ship passed through the Cape Verde Islands with slaves bound for Brazil. From Suriname to Cayenne, stories of slave women and children hiding rice seeds in their hair are legendary. African rice was a provision on slave ships to Brazil. By 1550, the rice was for sale in Rio de Janeiro. By 1618, it was a staple crop for enslaved Africans on sugar plantations in Brazil.

During the seventeenth century, Portuguese and Dutch forces fought for control of Brazil. As plantations developed, more slaves came from Africa. Asian rice arrived in 1766 and was planted for export. By 1781, all the rice consumed in Portugal was grown in Brazil. When Brazil declared independence in 1822, rice production continued as before and became a mainstay of the Brazilian diet. As cities grew, so did rice consumption. This may partially explain why the national dish of Brazil, *feijoada completa*, includes beans, rice, smoked or barbecued meats, kale, orange slices and toasted manioc flour. Manioc is a Brazilian staple, although in recent years its consumption has declined.

Tens of thousands of runaway slaves set up *quilombo* settlements in the dense Maranhâo rainforests. They farmed rice, maize, manioc and bananas and hunted fish and land animals. After slavery was abolished in Brazil in 1888, some slaves left for the cities, while descendants of the original *quilombo* inhabitants still farm rice there today.

When slavery ended legally in Latin America in the late 1800s, new sources of labour were needed for the colonial estates, *haciendas* and plantations, and for building railroads. Organized Asian immigrant convoys to Latin and South America included Chinese, Japanese and East Indian labourers, predominantly men. The Japanese settled in Peru and Brazil, the East Indians went to the British West Indies. Significant numbers of Chinese men left to settle in Brazil, Peru, Cuba and Mexico, where they married local women and adopted their culinary traditions.

'Guinea' (African) rice had been imported to Europe by the end of the fifteenth century by the Portuguese; it was not yet a staple, and more rice was needed. In the 1730s, Portugal imported rice both from Italy and South Carolina, to supplement rising demand for rice in Catholic Europe, which often

Costa Rican rice tamales.

accompanied fish on holy days (there were at least 100 holy days each year). Persistent cereal shortages in Europe led to rising imports. Brazilian rice seemed to be the answer. Only later was Asian rice planted for export. Rice in Africa was thought to be Asian in origin (even Linnaeus thought this). In Africa rice was brought by Portuguese traders and deposited on the Upper Guinea coast (hence the term 'Guinea rice'). Botanical evidence from the twentieth century confirms that African rice was cultivated at least 4,500 years ago, long before Europeans ventured onto the 'dark continent'. This red rice grew in French West Africa and was an independent species, despite the Eurocentric view that Europe brought rice culture to West Africa and the Americas. When 'Carolina White' rice arrived in Portugal in 1766, to be shipped to Brazil, Italian rice of African origin had already been shipped to be planted. While husking mills removed the exterior of the rice grain, pestles and mortars were still in use until 1774 because of a shortage of mechanical mills. Birds – a major nuisance – dropped seeds from one rice species onto the fields of another, thus making grain separation almost impossible. African rice was finally outlawed and Asian rice took over.

Britain and India

The British began trading in India in the early seventeenth century, with commerce peaking during the Raj era (1858–1947). Cross-currents between British and Indian gastronomy moved mainly in the direction of Britain, and were accelerated by Indian immigration. Rice started being introduced into the country by returning Anglo officials as well as the Indian seamen who had remained in Britain. The arrival of Indian restaurants and takeaways, as well as the manufacture of processed Indian foods and their increasing convenience, has made British-Indian foods ubiquitous.

From the mid-1800s onward, Britain was the gateway through which rice was taxed before leaving for European ports. Asian rice became increasingly important after the American Civil War cut off rice exports from former British

An Anglo-Indian breakfast: Victorian print illustrating the manner and customs of the Indians and the Anglo-Indians, including rice and fish.

Rice pilaf.

colonies. Revolutions in Europe increased demand for rice. Some rice stayed in Britain to accommodate Indian immigrants, a continuing trend that now includes recent Chinese, Southeast Asian and African-Caribbean immigrants. By the early nineteenth century military officials and administrators in India referred to themselves as Anglo-Indians. 'Nabobs' were wealthy British men who served during the Raj and returned home after independence in 1947. They often brought their Indian cooks with them. Indian seamen, especially cooks from Bangladesh, came to Britain in the early twentieth century and opened small restaurants. From curry houses to pubs to Veeraswamy's, an Indian restaurant opened by the Anglo-Indian Edward Palmer in 1926 that is still going strong, British versions of Indian food were easily found. While they were not very similar to the meals eaten in India, rice was the common link, and 'curry rice' became the most popular dish. 'Curry rice' is usually served with white rice, unadorned. Fragrant pilafs and biryanis, cardamom-scented rice pudding and kabobs with saffron rice; these dishes are also part of the Anglo-Indian experience.

Indian puffed rice with molasses – the precursor of Rice Krispie Treats?

Originally intended for their immigrant compatriots, Indian restaurants soon attracted British Raj-nostalgic men and women. As the desire for Indian flavours increased, a facsimile of Indian food became the norm. Chicken tikka masala, a British invention, is perhaps the most well known.

Jars of chutneys, pickles, curry mixes and ready-to-use sauces such as tikka masala and vindaloo are commonly found in supermarkets and department stores today. Rice – from Patna to Bengal to Basmati – is readily available. In the freezer are myriad ready-to-heat-and-eat meals, as well as boil-in-the-bag or microwave meals that can be spooned directly onto hot rice.

The British taste for 'Indian food' does not sufficiently explain its great popularity in Britain. A tradition of using spices during medieval times already existed in Britain (among the wealthy, at least) and may help to explain why strong seasonings were so easily adopted by the British, although this idea is controversial. The number of Indian restaurants in Britain exploded after the Second World War and may represent a consequence of rationing, which did not end until the 1950s. Small restaurants became a pathway through which immigrants sustained themselves while assimilating. According to Colleen Taylor Sen in *Curry: A Global History* (2009), the word 'curry' should be applied only to dishes developed in British Indian kitchens. So where does rice fit in? Rarely mentioned but always assumed, a mound of steaming white rice enhanced the consumption of Anglo-Indian culture in Britain, grain by grain.

An excellent example of cross-culinary pollination is kedgeree (English spelling). This rice and lentil dish, called *khichri* in Hindi, is everyday fare for millions of Indians. Thought of as too low-class for British tables, it was 'elevated' to higher status by the inclusion of smoked fish and hard-boiled eggs, an early indication of the middle-class desire for animal protein. It is still served at elegant British lunches.

Indonesia

From the mid-1400s the Dutch and Portuguese alternately fought for control of the Maluku Islands (formerly the Spice Islands, also called Moluccas), the rest of the Indonesian Islands and Sri Lanka. The Maluku Islands traded in pepper, nutmeg, cloves, mace and ginger, which were immensely profitable goods. The Dutch East India Company was begun in 1602 in order to better control trade: as a result Dutch influence became dominant. As with the British in India, the attempts by the colonizers to distance themselves from the colonized became evident at the table. Rice, vegetables and soup were standard fare for the islands' natives, especially on Java, where there was a strong Dutch presence. The extravagant *rijsttafel* – the rice table – was 'invented' by the Dutch, who sought to make their dining experience more European (or 'sophisticated') by adding many small plates of cooked and raw foods, sauces and condiments, even fried bananas. The *rijsttafel* was a way to show off one's status, and became a traditional Sunday meal. The connection to Indonesian eating habits was one of scale. For the Dutch, having many accompaniments was the point: many dishes signified status of one's colonizing clan, and rice played the role of both sidekick and palate cleanser. *Rifsttafel* restaurants are common in the Netherlands today and appeal to both Dutch and Indonesian people living there. However, *rijsttafel* is not generally cooked or eaten by Indonesians living in Indonesia.

4

The Rise of the Consumer

Rice is all one, but there are many ways of cooking it.
Swahili proverb

By 2050, cities will feed 70 per cent of the world population, which will by then have reached 9 billion. Urbanization changes how people acquire and eat rice. Rice provisioning and consumption habits have changed to accommodate these trends. Whether at home or at work, at food courts, corporate cafeterias or restaurants, convenience is the key to this story. While the growing middle classes show a reduction in their consumption of starchy staples in favour of animal protein, affordable rice takes up more and more shelf space in the supermarket.

From the mega mart to the corner bodega, processed rice products flourish as canned, bagged, boxed, chilled, frozen and microwave-ready items. From white to black to wild (which is not really rice at all, since it does not come from the *Oryza* genus but is a semi-annual aquatic grass, *Zizania aquatica*), partially processed rice products can be the consumer's foundation for urban meal preparation. In this chapter I will primarily focus on the consumption of rice in the U.S., but we must remember that each product derives from older, more distant,

Rice Council ad, 'My man likes something unexpected…', *c.* 1970s. Sex sells – even rice!

heritages and from more pastoral preparations, and can be found in other parts of the world as well.

Influential Immigrants

'Spanish rice', which included onions, peppers and tomatoes (the inclusion of other ingredients in the definition is more controversial) was common during the expansion of the U.S.

in the second half of the nineteenth century, when Texas, California and the Southwest were annexed, conquered or purchased, and the Mexicans living there became 'Americans' by default. The Mexican diet already included rice, which arrived with the Spanish in the 1520s (the Spanish also brought rice from the Philippines via the Pacific Ocean). Today, you can buy 'Spanish rice' in a box.

Italian immigrants were well established in the U.S. by the early twentieth century. Risotto, once exclusively prepared in Italian homes and later in restaurants, can now be bought in a processed format. American arborio rice is presently grown in California, Missouri and Arkansas. I was recently able to purchase a box of risotto alfredo, inspired by fettuccine alfredo. Made with organic California arborio rice, the preparation is simple and quick, requiring butter and milk. The rest of the ingredients are already in the box: rice, Parmesan cheese, salt, dairy powders, aromatics, spices and oil. The cooking time is 20 minutes, less than half the time of traditional risotto. Four servings cost $3.49.

The Asian immigrant population in the U.S. will reach 20 million by 2020. Recent arrivals have come from Hong Kong, Taipei, Malaysia, Fujian province in China, the Philippines and South Asia. While immigrants' offspring adapt to a more American diet, including an increased consumption of fast food, rice is still often cooked traditionally at home, particularly for weekend events, celebrations and festivals. There is a mix-and-match ethic as assimilation crosses with heritage lines. Asian entries in the 'ready meal' category represent another evolution in the market aisle. Lemon grass and rice noodle soup, or sushi wraps with sticky rice: both represent today's ready preparations. These products are found throughout the U.S., above all in California, New York and Texas: the states with the highest percentage of Asian immigrants.

Transportation and Trade

By the 1850s, the process of shipping goods was faster and less expensive thanks to trains and trucks. Refrigerated transport allowed semi-cooked products to move from point of origin to point of sale. As refrigerated planes and container ships joined the mix of transport options, the 'chill chain' – a method of temperature control that maintains freshness and safety of cooked food products – took rice-based meals from factory to refrigerated display case. As a result, cooked foods had a longer shelf life. Frozen foods improved in quality. Complete meals were part of the supermarket larder, only requiring reheating, if that.

Half of the world's rice is transported to cities. Factories and processing plants are often located in between the harvest country and consumption country. Modern rice factories are sometimes even located on land once formerly used as rice fields. Rice has evolved from a staple for survival into a processed product that responds to the shopper's preference and need for flavour, health, value and convenience. In addition, 40 per cent of American rice is used in beer production. Sake, miso and rice wine vinegar use fermented rice.

In my local supermarket in New York I recently purchased a packet of Tilda Thai Jasmine Rice. The rice is harvested in Thailand, milled and packaged in Britain and sold in the U.S., among other places. Modern trade agreements encourage such cross-country production and distribution because they generate cash for the exporting economy, despite problems with subsidies and international trade agreements. When prices are low, rice may be hoarded until the price increases. Thailand is a major rice exporter, especially of high-value Jasmine rice. Both Thai and American governments charge duties for rice imports, just as the British did during colonial times.

The way workers eat has changed. They no longer routinely eat lunch at home but bring it to work, or more likely, buy it. Whether in an aluminium container, eco-conscious paper container, plastic clamshell or Chinese takeaway container, the midday meal easily maintains food quality and temperature. Sushi and cold rice salads are ubiquitous: they are even now packaged in disposable bento boxes. Many offices now have microwave ovens in which lunch brought from home, purchased from a halal or Desi street cart, a food truck or a supermarket prepared-foods bar, a corporate cafeteria or in a restaurant, can be cooked or reheated. Delivery is standard. Tiffin 'ready meals' are delivered to Indian software engineers in Los Angeles, Toronto and London. This metal Anglo-Indian tiered lunch box, which usually includes rice, dal and curry, is delivered daily, just as it is in Indian cities. The recipients return yesterday's tiffin container for the next day's delivery. Tiffin containers don't require recycling. Could this be a trend?

Innovations

The invention of canning by French chemist Appert was the winning entry in a contest sponsored by Napoleon in the 1840s for safer and longer-lasting foods that could be transported to war zones. Canned cooked rice was eaten by American military troops, especially when added to soups and minced (ground) beef mixes, during the First World War.

Towards the end of the nineteenth century tinplate, used to make cans, was needed for military purposes other than those relating to food production, so other methods for preserving foods such as rice had to be developed. In 1879 came the folded paper box, invented by Robert Gair. Cardboard boxes had their advantages: the contents could be kept dry, fresh and had a long shelf life, they were well contained and lightweight. The package design and advertising enticed shoppers.

Innovations in refrigeration increased the food choices available to the consumer. Aseptic packaging and vacuum-sealed pouches continue to improve the texture and flavour of processed rice products. Pasteurization and other food safety processes paved the way for mass-market food production not only for supermarkets, but in meals-ready-to-eat – food in pouches that have their own heating elements – for the military. Schools, hospitals and prisons benefit from packaged, canned, frozen or microwaveable rice products. A signifier of this change lies in the u.s. Army manual. A version from 1906 uses canned rice, while another from 2006 refers to individual meals-ready-to-eat of Mexican rice, fried rice and Santa-Fe-style rice.

The locavore movement notwithstanding, we have evolved from consuming that which is grown nearby to that which is grown and shipped in from another country, with convenience and profit in mind. Rice and rice-based products can be ordered online and transported to anywhere in the world. While we associate these practices with economically developed countries, the same trends appear in urbanizing segments of Asia, South America and South Africa. 'Inclusive' packaged rice products make weekday life simple, and the desire for convenience has spread to newer immigrant groups, who may now save major cooking events only for weekends, holidays and festivals.

It is no surprise to learn that frozen rice meals are being manufactured in countries that have longstanding traditions of eating rice cooked in traditional ways. Competition in the commercial marketplace has countries like Thailand contemplating selling prepared frozen meals for shipment to the u.s. Britain is also considering shipping frozen Indian meals (the British version) to India's supermarkets, including chicken tikka masala. This 'added value' to a traditional export commodity will expand the global reach of prepared rice meals, and may just land on your table, wherever you are.

Some Iconic American Rice Products

In 2006 Americans spent 13 per cent of their income on food. Of this figure more than 40 per cent represents food that is eaten out (in comparison, African and Asian households spend 15–50 per cent of their food budgets on street food and eating out). The need for ready-to-eat or heat-and-eat food has accelerated as urban growth increases because new, smaller apartments are being built with mini kitchens, or communal kitchens on one floor (as in Portland, Oregon) and sometimes no kitchens at all, as in Hong Kong and Bangkok. Hotplates and microwave ovens are there to heat foods that are already completely prepared. And rice is a major player in this evolution.

The storeroom, or larder, was once used to stockpile the vegetables, canned, pickled, salted and dried meat, fish and fruit, which were needed to survive the winter. As cities grew, the 'room' disappeared and the 'store' arose. Most storeroom foods are now purchased, as opposed to being hunted or gathered, as in the past. Apartments with small kitchens and little storage space are the norm in cities, while houses in the suburbs have somewhat larger kitchens and more storage space (great places to store convenient packaged or frozen food).

Women entered the workforce in ever-greater numbers after the Second World War. From 1948 to 1985, women in the labour force rose from 29 to 45 per cent. In supermarkets, which at this time catered primarily to women, marketing

Quaker puffed rice, a popular breakfast cereal.

strategies proliferated to show how quick and easy it was to prepare rice, since women had less time to cook after they came home from work.

In 1904 puffed rice, 'shot out of cannons', was introduced at the St Louis World's Fair. The botanist and cereal inventor Alexander Pierce Anderson, who staged the stunt, knew that water in the precooked rice grain would turn to steam and expand through pressurized heat, thus puffing out the grain. The first commercially manufactured product in the U.S. using puffed rice, Rice Krispies cereal debuted in 1927. An early radio ad targeting children claimed the cereal would 'snap, crackle and pop' in a bowl of milk, and stay crunchy. Of course, puffed rice had been manufactured in India long before Rice Krispies came into existence, and is one ingredient in snacks of all kinds, including *mamra*, puffed rice seasoned with curry leaves, salt, sugar, turmeric, curry paste and garlic, heated until toasted. Similarly, *poha chevda* is puffed or flaked rice with fennel and sesame seeds, salt, sugar, oil and garlic.

The popular dessert/snack known as Rice Krispie Treats, made with melted marshmallows and butter, was introduced in 1941. Today, ready-to-eat Rice Krispie Treats are found individually packaged, and are sold at newsstands and super-markets. The commercially prepared version is one of the most requested snacks in the u.s. military. Rice Krispie Treats are sold in the United Kingdom, Europe, Canada and Australia.

In 1942, German chemist Eric Huzenlaub licensed his parboiling process to Gordon Harwell, who was selling 'Uncle Ben's Plantation Rice'. Parboiling involves pre-cooking the grain before polishing and pushes 80 per cent of the nutrients from the bran into the grain's centre, thus making white rice more nutritious. The American military became Harwell's chief customer and, by 1944, 20–30,000 tons of rice per year were produced, all for the war effort. After the war, Uncle Ben's Converted Rice was marketed in the u.s., Canada, Australia and Britain; it became the best-selling rice in the u.s., and is still the leading rice sold. Today there are all kinds of seasoned and pre-cooked Uncle Ben's rice combinations.

Puffed rice cereal: how to feed yourself!

Once again, precooked and dried rice in various forms has existed in India for generations; it is another old idea reinvented for a new market.

In 1958 Vince DeDomenico marketed an old family recipe of rice and vermicelli pasta, both sautéed in butter before being cooked in chicken broth. Armenian in origin, this recipe had its preparation methods in common with early versions of pilaf (first cooking rice in fat, then simmering in broth). DeDomenico's mass-marketed version involved a precooked dried rice and pasta mix in a box, with dried seasoning replacing the chicken broth. The only addition was water. Because the product was half rice and half pasta, DeDomenico called it Rice-A-Roni ('roni' like macaroni). The first advertising commercial featured San Francisco's cable cars and the famous jingle, 'The San Francisco Treat!'

Rice snacks: crispy, crunchy, colourful.

American rice cakes evolved from their Asian and Indian forebears. China and Japan have innumerable kinds of rice cakes and wafers: soft, hard, thin, thick, sweet, savoury. Whether soft, as in Indian *idlis* or crunchy as in Japanese *senbei*, the exact combination of time, temperature, high starch rice and water may produce a soft wrapping for sweet bean paste, a thin batter that can become a crêpe or a crispy, crunchy cracker. Another popular Japanese rice product is *mochi*, glutinous rice, steamed and pressed into cakes, filled with bean paste or ice cream. *Mochi* is found in freezers all over Japan and anywhere there is a Japanese community in the u.s.

One of the first producers of rice cakes in the u.s. is the Umeya Rice Cake Company, founded in 1924 by the Japanese Hamano brothers, for their own community. Despite internment of the founders in American detention camps during the Second World War, the company eventually rebounded and supplied shops all over the u.s. with the rice cakes. American rice crackers come in brown, white and mixed versions, are extolled for their low calorific value and high fibre (in the version that uses brown rice) and may be seasoned with Cheddar cheese, soy sauce, sesame or caramel.

Minute Rice was invented by Afghani Ataullah Ozai-Durrani and marketed by General Foods Corporation in 1949. From one product came many additions, including today's individual microwavable cups of cooked rice that take only one minute to cook. These rice meals come with package and online recipe suggestions that reflect the immigrant backgrounds of the American demographic. From curried rice to salsa rice to Asian chicken rice to Greek rice salad, whether you are bringing to life your own heritage or somebody else's, Minute Rice will help.

Instant rice noodle soup in a microwavable cup is advertised to workers, students, parents and the elderly, for a quick, easy, 'no dishes to wash' meal. Wheat and rice noodles were first pan-fried and dried, then added to Styrofoam cups and bowls with dried vegetables and a seasoning packet. Add boiling water and wait a minute or two. Invented in 1958 by Momofuku Ando, this soup in a cup was once voted the most popular Japanese food invention in Japan.

Restaurants

In eateries and restaurants, rice is ever-present. This was not always the case. As immigrants from rice-focused countries have increased in number in the u.s. and Europe, so too have eateries that cater to them, and to the rest of us. 'Authenticity' is not the point, although a close resemblance to 'the real thing' is always a good selling point, no matter how far-fetched the link.

During the 1850s, Chinese workers in California opened small, simple restaurants in their 'Chinatowns' in order to cater to their compatriots. Steamed white rice mounded in a bowl was the backdrop for pork, greens, tofu, seasonings of fermented black beans, soy and oyster sauces, as well as garlic, ginger, spring onions (scallions) and sesame oil. Eventually, menus expanded as non-Chinese customers arrived, although there was often a separation between what the Chinese and non-Chinese ate, with the exception of rice, of course!

What we think of as 'fried rice' began as a way to use up leftovers in the kitchen and was not included on the menu, at first at least. Nevertheless, fried rice in various guises (pork, shrimp, tofu) has become a staple in restaurants today, whether Cantonese or not. Fried rice is now available as Minute Rice, a ready-to-eat microwave meal.

Rice paper summer rolls: light, colourful, low-calorie –Vietnamese refreshment.

The Asian immigrants that came to New York, California and Texas beginning in the 1970s prepared rice that reflected their backgrounds. *Pho* – the archetypal Vietnamese rice noodle soup – is found in San Jose and Houston; Thai sticky rice with mangoes and coconut is eaten in Los Angeles and New York City; Fujianese chicken with fermented red rice paste can be found in Queens, New York and in Little Fuzhou, in Brooklyn, New York. Indonesian, Korean, Singaporean, Taiwanese and Malaysian rice dishes are also represented.

According to folklore, risotto emerged in Italy in 1574. A stained-glass maker, working on Il Duomo in Milan, added saffron to his glass recipe to achieve a bright yellow colour. Liking the results, as a joke, he also coloured the beef marrow and rice with saffron at a wedding feast, but the guests found the dish delectable. It became known as *risotto alla Milanese*. The classic way to make risotto involves cooking short-grain, high-starch rice in butter or oil, so that the grains are coated with fat. Hot stock or other liquids are added very slowly, and the mixture must be stirred continuously while the starch is slowly released from the grains, which acquire a chewy, creamy texture. Butter and grated Parmigiano-Reggiano cheese are added shortly before consuming. When risotto is featured on menus in Italian restaurants, there is often a caveat: 'The risotto will take 25 minutes to prepare.' In addition to the classic *risotto alla Milanese*, restaurant goers now find all kinds of risotto on the menu. Speedier ways to prepare risotto have evolved, and less traditional ingredients have become standard: vegetarian risotto with tofu, and non-dairy risotto (made with rice milk and puréed nuts for creaminess). Risotto now even comes in a box.

Paella originated in Valencia, Spain. The word 'paella' may be a corruption of the phrase *por ella*, which means 'for her'. (According to legend, a lover once prepared *por ella* for his fiancée.) Or, it may come from the name of the round, shallow pan with two handles that is used for cooking paella, a *paellera*. Paella began as a mixture of rice, vegetables, rabbit and snails that labourers cooked over an open fire in the fields and ate directly from the pan. A *soccarat* is formed when the bottom of the pan remains very hot and browns the bottommost rice, which becomes crunchy. In the u.s., *paella Valenciana* has come to mean a preparation that includes chicken, chorizo, shrimp, clams, short- or medium-grain white rice, vegetables and seasonings, and saffron. And yes, paella comes in a box or as a frozen meal.

Pilaf was originally destined for aristocrats. Called *pulao* in Iran, Afghanistan and India, the best pilaf is made with aromatic Basmati rice that is usually aged for several years, and therefore is expensive. The goal of every pilaf cook is to serve fragrant mounds of steaming individual rice grains. To make pilaf, rice is washed or soaked, then drained until the water runs clear of starch. A spice mix of pounded green cardamom pods, cumin seeds and cloves is cooked in ghee with caramelized onions. Rice is stirred into the mixture and the grains are coated with fat. Water or stock is added, and the rice cooks at a simmer until 'steam holes' appear. Then the covered pot steams for another 20 to 30 minutes. Putting a dry towel on top of the rice, inside the pot, helps absorb the water condensing on the inner lid and ensures that the grains will continue to separate from each other. This prevents gummy rice. Afghans and Iranians often pour ghee into the centre of cooked rice where it spreads across the bottom of the pot. As the rice steams for 30 more minutes, a *tahdig* is formed: a browned crunchy crust on the bottom of the pot.

While the origins of gumbo will be forever debated, there are some facts that are not in dispute: they may seem contradictory, but that is part of the story. Gumbo is the essential Creole (for some) or Cajun (for others) soupy rice dish that gets its name from okra (from the Bantu word *nkombo*). The legacy of French colonialism includes roux, a butter or oil and flour mixture used for thickening. Some gumbos use ground sassafras as a thickener; a Choctaw influence. Cajuns use crawfish in their gumbos. Spicy sausages may have come from the Cajuns, and smoked sausage from the Germans. The use of tomatoes depends on the cook and her or his traditions.

The Street

Street food is the most convenient food. Found at stalls and carts, food trucks and outdoor markets or festivals, it has evolved into the 'ethnic' fast food found in food courts, where Chinese, Indian, Thai and Mexican restaurants set up shop. Anything wrapped, stuffed or easy to eat is suitable street food. You can indulge in crispy, sugar-coated Yunnan strawberries wrapped in rice paper in the Chinese city of Kunming, or gorge on goat biryani in Mumbai in India. How about

Korea-town (in New York) *kimbap*: steamed rice, stuffed with pickled radish or tuna, rolled in toasted seaweed sheets? Or *bolinhos de arroz*: rice fritters stuffed with sardines and cheese in Rio de Janeiro? Or in New Orleans *calas*, fried dough balls made with cooked rice and sprinkled with powdered sugar.

Some street foods require more than one's hands. *Pho*, Vietnamese rice noodle soup, Tex-Mex *carne asada* with rice and beans, or Gambian chicken *Yassa* with rice: these foods are derived from Vietnam, Texas and Gambia, but are also found in New York, New Mexico and California, courtesy of the immigrant presence there.

Street food can be an inexpensive and practical way to feed one's family. In southern China, huge pyramids of *chong* pile up in bamboo steamers. Consumers unwrap the banana-leaf-wrapped rice balls filled with seasoned mushrooms and eat them piping hot. Coconut-scented packets of *puso*, jasmine rice wrapped in boiled coconut fronds, fit the bill in Luzon in the Phillippines. In southern India, *idli*, puffy, light-as-air steamed rice-and-lentil cakes, are a common breakfast food, and let's not forget *dosas*, those fermented rice and lentil 'crêpes' that enclose curried vegetables or potatoes with mustard seed, among many variations. In Indonesia, street fare might be *nasi goreng*, fried rice flavoured with *belacan* (shrimp paste) and shredded cooked egg.

Street carts and food trucks abound. They bring their rice meals to busy neighbourhoods, food festivals, farmers' markets and agricultural fairs. These movable feasts offer vegetable kormas with spiced basmati rice, or Korean fried rice with *kim chi* and pork. The Kogi BBQ truck in Los Angeles, which started the food truck movement, has recently opened a restaurant: the reverse of the usual scenario. What is served? Korean rice bowls, with meatballs, pork belly or tofu, and Korean pickles.

Sushi: A Special Scenario

Sometimes, street food is elaborate and expensive; at other times, simple and cheap. Sushi, too, can be either.

It is thought that during the second century CE near the Mekong River, in landlocked parts of China, Laos and northern Thailand, salted fish was placed between layers of cooked rice. The container was sealed for a lengthy period of time, during which the salt, and rice fermentation, preserved the fish. The rice was discarded before consuming the fish, although a few aficionados enjoyed the intense aroma (much like blue cheese). The preparation time and costs involved made this food for the wealthy. For those who lived near the water, acquiring fish was much easier.

This sushi style migrated to China and Japan in the seventh century. The Japanese ate the rice and the fish, while the Chinese did not take to it. Increasing popularity for this rice/fish combination in Japan resulted in shorter preservation times, so as to keep up with demand. While the fish was still protected from bacterial contamination, the rice became

Sushi.

much more palatable. In 718 CE, sushi was acceptable to the government as a form of tax payment. By the early seventeenth century, sushi rice was seasoned with a revolutionary new product: vinegar made from rice, 'rice wine vinegar' (which actually has nothing to do with wine). Seasoning the rice with rice wine vinegar permitted fish and rice to be eaten together because the rice wine mimicked the flavour of fermented rice, and had preservative qualities as well. Sushi consumption had also become much less expensive and more democratic, moving from the aristocracy to the labourers who frequented street markets at lunchtime. Simple rice and fish combinations as well as elaborate bento boxes of prepared sushi, with pickles and other condiments, were ready to be eaten anytime.

After the Second World War, sushi stalls and carts in Japan were moved indoors to more sanitary conditions. As Japanese restaurants proliferated, sushi began its global migration while adapting to newer environments, giving rise to the California roll, the inside-out roll and sushi with brown rice. Top sushi chefs are very particular about which rice they use, and some even polish their own rice (top-grade short- or medium-grain rice). Apprentice sushi chefs begin their long training by learning to prepare rice.

Sushi is served from high-end restaurants to institutional cafeterias, and can be purchased at supermarkets and at stores that sell only pre-packaged sushi. This style of sushi is prepared in factories where robots mould the rice into individual oblongs or rolls. Trained staff add sliced fish. The use of frozen farmed fish and lesser-quality rice has brought the price of sushi down from food for the wealthy to food for the masses. As a result, sushi is almost global in its reach. Some sushi restaurants use conveyor belts that move around a circular counter: customers take small plates as they pass by.

Perhaps the best example of the sushi explosion is in São Paulo, Brazil, which has an abundance of sushi restaurants. Japanese immigrants first came to work in this area on coffee plantations in 1908. The Japanese population grew, and today São Paulo has the largest such community outside of Japan. Seventeen million sushi meals are eaten every month. In Brazil, sushi began as a luxury product for wealthy diners. As its popularity increased, automation of rice and fish brought the price down. Cafeterias and salad bars now offer sushi. One change that reflects the background of Brazil's history with rice is the preference for serving long-grain rice with Japanese foods other than sushi. Outside of Asia, Brazil has one of the highest consumptions of rice: 40 kg (88 lb) per person annually. And sushi is often prepared using Brazilian ingredients to reflect local tastes: mango, strawberry and raw beef.

Sake

Fermented rice and water combinations have existed in China and Korea for millennia, but Japanese sake – the one with which we are most familiar – began about 2,500 years ago. Moulds, fermentation and wild yeasts, and the even earlier chew-and-spit technique, were used to ferment brown rice and water into gruels that were strained. The resulting brew was light brown and cloudy. In AD 689, the new brewing department at the Imperial Palace, along with Chinese help, developed moulds that increased alcohol content. The ritualistic aspect of sake drinking solidified when Shinto monasteries became legal breweries in their own right. During the next 400 years, sake brewing became a business. Kyoto and Kobe became major brewing centres. Government taxes ensued. In the late 1500s, when rice began to be polished, sake could be

Sake.

made either cloudy or clear. By the 1800s, just as with single malt scotch, wine and cheese, local conditions – including time of year, rice type, terrain, climate and water – influenced the flavour of sakes, and local sakes came to be preferred by different consumers. During periods of rice shortage (the Second World War, for example), mixing a small amount of rice with distilled cheap alcohol produced low-quality sakes. After the Second World War, whiskies, wine and beer became popular in Japan, while sake became more popular in Europe, South America, Australia and the u.s.

Sake came to Hawaii in 1885 with Japanese labourers on sugar plantations. Import taxes kept increasing, so Japanese-owned breweries were built on American soil. Initially intended to increase sales, lesser-quality sake was produced. This sake was heated, which helped disguise its poor quality. Other deviations from Japanese etiquette included drinking sake with sushi. Not only does traditional sushi etiquette dictate that sake not be drunk with sushi ('like with like' is frowned upon in some etiquette circles), but high-quality sake should be served chilled, with vintages and other labelling information available to connoisseurs.

The Electric Rice Cooker

Rice is usually simmered, boiled (like pasta), steamed over water or cooked with a combination of these methods. Any of these techniques may result in imperfectly cooked rice, especially for rice cooked in a pot and requiring one to tend to the flame or coal and adjust the rice by moving the pot and rice around. While reliable gas stoves have existed for more than a century, the rice cooker revolutionized rice cooking in Japan, and from there, the world.

The first automatic rice cooker was manufactured by Toshiba in 1955. A rice cooker that kept rice warm all day was introduced in 1960, and became wildly popular. Sushi restaurants also greatly benefited. In 1979 digital technology allowed one to set a timer the night before and have hot rice for breakfast. In 1988, Matsushita introduced induction heat cookers. While slow to catch on, they now comprise more than half of rice cooker sales, despite being more expensive. The advantages include not having to soak the rice and, with a gentle stir at the

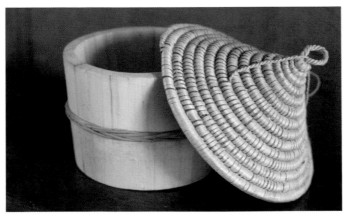

Contemporary rice steamer in Yunnan: I brought it back to New York, where it works very well.

Today's electronic rice cooker.

end (which lets excess moisture evaporate), a more consistent product. In 2003, Matsushita introduced a rice cooker that also uses very hot steam: this makes the rice more aromatic.

Matsushita has found sufficient interest in rice cookers in Europe and the u.s. to produce specialized rice cookers tailored to customers' preferences. In the u.s., a basket above the cooker is included, for steaming vegetables. The lid is transparent so you can see when everything is ready. Rice cookers vary depending on which rice you prefer, whether it is parboiled and whether you steam or boil it. Rice cookers, just like rice, have adapted to the needs of their audience.

5
Art, Ritual and Symbolism

Luck is like having a rice dumpling fly into your mouth.
Japanese proverb

Rice has inspired origin myths, customs, rituals, language and attitudes. Sometimes traditions have developed into newer paradigms after people migrate, or when modern technology is implemented. Pesticides replace prayers, and rapid-growth rice supersedes traditional varieties. Modern technology in rice production is also the source of lost traditions and increasing unemployment, as machines replace humans.

Attempts to save on labour with research into direct seeding, mechanical rice transplanters, weedicide screening, and mechanical threshing are conducive to despair as a use of aid funds in Asian research centres. The issue is largely a matter of timing. As economies grow, the point is reached where there is no longer a surplus but a shortage of labour in the agricultural sector ... The unmistakable trend is marked by the gradual disappearance in many regions of practices and techniques that have been used for centuries in the production of rice. The tractor is replacing the water buffalo for land preparation; direct seeding of rice is replacing transplanting; herbicides are replacing hand weeding; the mechanical thresher is replacing traditional hand threshing of the paddy … While the youth no longer look to rice farming as a way of life, those left behind to tend the rice fields are adopting new practices to lighten the burden and increase the productivity of their labours.

Despite the changes discussed above in 'Rice Research and Production in the 21st Century', a report by IRRI in 2001, ancient traditions are valued and rituals are maintained when it comes to rice. Religious shrines are found in rice paddies and religious harvest ceremonies are common. The Water Puppets of Hanoi theatre fame mimic rice planting, and harvest symbolism, in their performances. Followers of Mae Posop, the Thai rice goddess, discreetly cut rice stalks when harvesting them so as not to offend her. Baskets of rice are poured over

Hong Kong airport: be happy, eat rice?

Rice shrine in the paddy.

the heads of Indian brides and grooms. Handfuls of rice are tossed at American weddings as well (although in America birdseed is now thrown instead if the ceremony is held outdoors, since birds cannot digest raw rice). There is some overlap in myth origin stories; this makes sense when you understand the complex way rice moved from people to people, and land to land.

Not all rice imagery is life-affirming, however. Rice grains and rice agriculture have been metaphorically used to negatively denote racial and gender distinctions.

Origin Stories and Myths: Gods and Rice

Dietary staples usually have a variety of origin myths. Frequently, gods are credited with giving or withholding basic foods: wine, beer, corn, chocolate, wheat and rice have all been implicated. To encourage abundant harvests, people worship at shrines and temples, and make offerings to male and female deities, whether human or animal. An abundant rice harvest not only guarantees immediate survival, but is also a hedge against future privation.

Some gods are vengeful and even feel guilt. The Javanese story of Tisnawati is illustrative. Tisnawati, a god's daughter, falls in love with the mortal Jakasudana. Tisnawati's father does not approve of the relationship between god and mortal. As punishment, Tisnawati is changed into a rice stalk. Later, her father takes pity on her lover, and turns him into a rice stalk as well, placing him next to his beloved. Their union is re-enacted at the harvest festival, and symbolizes the triumph of committed love over more temporal and less reliable emotions.

Commitment, a willingness to work very hard and choreographed teamwork are required for a good rice harvest, and these three elements may produce an affinity for mathematical reasoning, as Malcolm Gladwell points out in his book *Outliers: The Story of Success* (2008). While this is a stereotype (hence its inclusion in 'Gods and Myths'), Gladwell points out that rice paddies in Southern China are very small, and the whole family gets involved in all aspects of rice agriculture. The timing of plantings, square footage, land maintenance, water levels, a level claypan, weeding, irrigating and all the other labour-intensive parts of rice farming are still manual. Decisions are made daily and many involve arithmetic and fractions. Add to this the more rapidly developed memory skills of younger Chinese in terms of numbers (compared to Americans), and the hours spent working (both in the paddy and in the classroom and at home) and you have an explanation for Asian success in American mathematics classes. Singapore, China (Taiwan), South Korea, Hong Kong and Japan are linked through wet rice agriculture and specialization in mathematics.

Other gods are generous. In Tamil Nadu in India the rice goddess is Ponniamman. The name is an amalgamation of the name of the 'Ponni' rice that grows in the area and the Tamil word for goddess, *amman*. Heavy flooding frequently washed away rice fields in the region. A statue of Ponniamman was erected, prayers were offered and the floods abated.

A Chinese rice-origin myth tells the story of a people who had taken refuge in the mountains after floods destroyed their plants. A dog ran by with rice panicles hanging from its tail (the panicle is part of the rice tiller that bears rice spikelets, which develop into grains). The seeds fell to the ground as the dog ran, and rice shoots grew where the seeds fell.

Also in China, a mythical hunter named Houh Jir had five sons. He gave each one a sack to fill with one of the five staples: hemp, wheat, millet, beans and rice. The son who filled the bag with rice was named Pahdi: this was the origin of rice, and it became known as 'paddy' in honour of the son.

Bulul figure, Philippines: please fill that bowl with rice to cook for my family.

On the rice terraces of the Ifugao in the Philippines, bulol figures, in male and female pairs, represent rice gods. The god Humidhid made four carvings in human form, from the dark wood of narra tree, a national symbol of the Philippines. The statuettes went downriver, where they multiplied and protected the rice paddies and the granaries where rice is stored.

Inari, the Japanese rice god, is thought to have cultivated the first rice plant. While a snake guarded a bale of rice, a fox came along to do his bidding, which included dropping rice seeds to be planted. Families often have small shrines to Inari at home, and Shinto and Buddhist shrines celebrate Inari. Also called the 'God of Prosperity', Inari stands on two bags of rice while riding the fox. There are numerous variants on this theme.

Celebrations: A Rice Festival Sampler

In Bali, the harvest festivals honours the goddess of rice, Dewi Sri, in three forms: Tiswanati, the goddess who gave birth to rice, and whom we have met before in Java; Mae Posop, the goddess who protects the rice crops (she is also the Thai rice goddess); and finally, harvested rice that appears as a mortal woman. One story explains the origin of the rice plant this way: the god Batara Guru was given an egg-shaped jewel. When he opened it, he found a beautiful young girl, whom he named Tisnawati. All were heartbroken when she died as a young woman. After her burial, the king was riding in the forest. Near Tiswanati's grave, he saw a beautiful shining light. As he came closer, he found that a coconut palm grew from her head, the banana tree from her hands, corn from her teeth, and rice from her genitals.

During festivals, villages are repainted and decorated with flags. Rice-god statuettes dusted with rice flour that honour Dewi Sri are placed throughout the fields. Models of the mother spirit made from rice sheaves are hung near paddies to ensure good crops. Granaries are the dwellings of ancestral spirits, so they are often built to look like small houses, in which ancestors have enough rice to eat until the next harvest. Ceremonial objects, usually made by the senior woman of the household, are placed in the granary. Meals of spit-roasted duck and pig are eaten with *nasi goreng* (fried rice), rice sweets and dumplings.

Dewi Sri: Thai rice goddess made of rice straw.

Pongal rice art: multicoloured rice-powder designs set the stage for the annual Pongal rice festival.

The state of Tamil Nadu hosts a four-day Hindu harvest called Pongal to give thanks to the sun, rainfall, cattle and cereal grains – rice in particular – as well as for sugarcane and turmeric. On day one, people light a huge bonfire at dawn and throw old and unused items into the fire. They clean their homes and decorate the ground outside the entrances with elaborately coloured rice-powder designs. The farmers anoint their ploughs and sickles with sandalwood paste before using them to cut the newly harvested rice. The sun god, Lord Surya, is honoured on day two. He is offered rice that has been cooked in milk in an earthenware pot and decorated with turmeric and sugarcane. When the pot boils over, devotees share the cooked rice. Buffaloes and cows are washed, garlanded with flowers, and worshipped on day three to give thanks for ploughing the fields. They also eat rice boiled in milk. On day four, young women prepare and leave balls of cooked rice out in the fields for the birds to eat. The Pongal festival is considered propitious for marriages, as those with a plentiful harvest can supply rice and other necessities for the wedding.

The June rice-planting festival in Osaka, Japan, reproduces ancient rituals. The paddies are still tilled by oxen. In larger cities, rice is sometimes planted on the rooftops of skyscrapers. Performing spectacular dances and singing special songs invigorates the grains and reinforces beliefs that spirits live in the rice seedlings, which must be planted in Mother Earth. The women sing and dance while wearing *kasa* (braided hats) festooned with flowers, while a procession of samurai warriors clad in full armour passes by. The highlight is the *Sumiyoshi Odori* dance by 150 young girls. Participants' prayers are answered with the autumn rice harvest. Once harvested, rice offerings are made to the shrine deities in October and, on 23 November, a ceremony is held to express thanks for the bounty.

The ceremony of naming the child on the 11th day after it is born, *c.* 1820, from an album illustrating the lives of Brahmins. Ladies of the house are being served at the back, and the men and invited Brahmins at the front. Each has a plantain leaf as a plate, with a mound of rice, dosa, vegetables with tea and cups.

In China, the La Ba Rice Porridge Festival, Spring Festival (Chinese New Year), Dragon Boat Festival and Mid-Autumn Festival are only a few of the festivals that celebrate the importance of rice in everyday life: the arrival of new rice, a plentiful harvest, the solstice and, in our example, matchmaking. At the Guizhou Sister Meal Festival, Sister Rice is a culinary and symbolic key. The intensely coloured rice is made by young women who collect leaves, flowers and grass to make coloured water, in which they soak the rice for a few days. They put tokens in the rice and give them to Sister Rice to hand out to young men that catch their eye. The rice colour and the token indicate different interests. Red rice, for example, means that the village from which the woman comes is flourishing. If cotton is found within the rice, the woman is showing her eagerness to marry, if garlic, the opposite is true.

A more contemporary honour takes place in Mengzi County, Yunnan province, in southwest China, and celebrates a dish called Crossing Bridge rice noodles. The story is said to have arisen from a wife's efforts to provide her husband with hot lunches, while he studied for exams on a quiet island in Nanhu Lake, far from home. His wife came with lunch every day, but by the time she crossed the bridge to reach him, the soup was cold. One day, she made chicken soup. When she arrived at her husband's study, the soup was still steaming hot: it had an insulating layer of chicken fat floating on top, and this kept the soup warm enough to last the long trip. As a result, chicken soup became the foundation of the meal, rather than the meal itself. Various thinly sliced, uncooked ingredients, such as rice noodles, meat, fish and vegetables would also accompany the soup. These items would be tossed into the scalding soup just before eating it, ensuring a fresh and hot meal.

Crossing Bridge noodles, Yunnan: a story of devotion, both marital and scholarly.

Korean rice candy sold on the streets of Seoul: toasty, sweet, chewy and crunchy.

In both North and South Korea, noodles (symbolic of long life) and dumplings are often served on birthdays. Steamed glutinous rice cakes are flavoured with chestnuts, honey, jujubes, sorghum and mugwort. Especially favoured in South Korea, rice cakes flavoured with mugwort leaves are supposed to have therapeutic value. These cakes are traditionally served at the Tano festival.

During the early Choson dynasty (1390 to 1910, but especially during the sixteenth and seventeenth centuries) and concomitant rise of Confucianism, holiday rituals and seasonal festivals flourished. Harmony with nature was encouraged through the consumption of rice-cake soup, rice cakes steamed on pine needles, sweet rice beverages and more. Rice-cake soup was eaten on New Year's Day. And on a child's one hundredth day of life, he or she would receive steamed rice cakes, which represent innocence and purity. On the child's first birthday, a layered rainbow rice cake might symbolize his or her future endeavours.

Rice is significant in many West African ceremonies. While women are the primary field workers, various rituals include masquerades performed by men, with masks and headdresses that mimic animals and birds. Feasts that use rice as the centre of the meal support the link between rice and women's fertility. Elaborate woodcarvings and winnowing baskets made from reeds and other grasses are also part of these rituals. The baskets are still made in Africa, and can also be found in the Low Country of South Carolina today.

To promote a good harvest in Liberia and on the Ivory Coast, Dan women dance with wooden rice ladles carved to portray animals and people, while in Mali, Bamana men wear antelope headdresses and dance to the spirits. At Baga weddings in Guinea and Liberia, brides dance with baskets on their heads, into which onlookers toss gifts of rice and money.

In the U.S., Arkansas, Louisiana, South Carolina and Texas all have annual rice festivals. The festival is a time to celebrate the harvest, eat lots of good food made with rice and highlight the importance of the rice industry to the community. The International Rice Festival in Crowley, Louisiana, includes a parade, a ceremony that involves crowning the 'rice king' and 'rice queen' and rice eating and rice cooking contests. Every kind of rice-based food is available, from boudins (a sausage made with rice), to jambalaya to gumbo.

The Texas Rice Festival is an annual harvest celebration held in October, around the town of Winnie, Texas. The event features a carnival and parades, a livestock and longhorn show, a horse show, barbecue cook-off, nightly street dances, rice cooking contest, pageants and features food made with rice and flavours of Cajun culture, which is strong in the area. Typical fare includes rice balls, gumbo, *étouffée* (often crawfish and other shellfish in a dark roux-enhanced sauce, served over rice), crab balls, boudin balls (sausage and rice balls) and funnel cakes, as well as cowboy casserole – a one-pot recipe that ordinarily includes minced (ground) beef, vegetables, beans and tomatoes, with biscuits or cornbread or rice, all cooked at the same time.

Beginning in 1976, the Arkansas Rice Festival included choosing a Miss Arkansas Rice Queen every year. All sorts of rice cooking contests take place and draw famous local chefs to demonstrate their skills. Rice is even eaten with butter and sugar (which incidentally was one of the prophet Muhammad's favourite dishes).

Paella is the star of the Fiesta del Arroz (Rice Festival) in Sueca, an agricultural town south of Valencia in Spain. This annual festival occurs during September and celebrates the most internationally known rice dish of Spain. Local and international chefs compete in the 'international paella contest' using the famous local rice, including *La Bomba* and other special short-grain rices that have rounded as well as long grains, and are especially absorptive. Valencia paella is traditionally made with chicken, rabbit, land snails and greens, although every village is proud of its own version. The most popular specialities are paella with chicken or rabbit, seafood paella or a mixed version. Among fishermen, *arroz a banda* evolved, so called because the rice and the fish are cooked separately, to fully develop the flavour of each part. It is served with aioli (garlic mayonnaise). Rice baked in earthenware pots with beetroot (beets), cuttlefish, cauliflower or spinach is also popular.

Cultural Customs and Rice Rituals

Showering brides and grooms with rice is an ancient ritual used by Assyrians, Hebrews and Egyptians. In a Hindu wedding ceremony, the bride's brother pours unhusked rice into the hands of the bride and groom as they walk around a fire. The couple offers this rice to the fire. Rice is the first food a new Indian bride gives to her husband and is also the first solid food eaten by an Indian infant. Rice and fertility are almost synonymous.

At Japanese weddings, rice cakes embossed with cranes or turtles are offered to the bride and groom as a symbol of longevity. Red beans and rice are given as gifts at a child's birth, while at Buddhist funerals, puffed rice is used to symbolize rice that cannot be grown again. At Korean funerals, three spoonfuls of rice are placed in the deceased person's mouth, along with some money, to ease the transition into the next world.

Language, Literature, and Art

The words 'rice', 'food', 'meal' and 'eat' are almost equal in several Asian languages. 'Agriculture' and 'rice' are often used synonymously. In myriad ways, rice is a vehicle of expression.

There are no references to rice in the Bible, but Confucius and Muhammad both considered rice as their favourite food. Muhammad liked rice cooked in ghee (clarified butter), often sweetened. Buddha, when he was still Siddhartha, was a man of many pleasures who turned to asceticism while seeking enlightenment. For many months, he lived on one grain of rice per day. One day, a young girl brought him a dish of rice cooked in milk. Restored, he was able to continue his quest. Buddha had rice-paddy designs sewn into his robes, designs still used today.

Devotees of Krishna were told that foods were divided into three categories, of which the first category includes rice, milk and dairy products, all aligned with virtue.

Many proverbs and sayings feature rice as the vehicle for conveying meaning or sentiment:

Don't let an angry man wash dishes; don't let a hungry man guard rice.
— *Cambodian proverb*

If you are planning for a year, sow rice; if you are planning for a decade, plant trees; if you are planning for a lifetime, educate people.
— *Chinese proverb*

Try to seize the bowl of rice but forget the whole table of food.
— *Vietnamese proverb*

Rice is born in water and must die in wine.
— *Italian proverb*

Have you eaten rice yet?
— *Traditional Thai greeting*

The great American jazz trumpeter Louis Armstrong's favourite food was red beans and rice. In tribute to this iconic dish from New Orleans, he signed his letters, 'Red beans and ricely yours'.

Another Side of Rice Symbolism

The phrase 'broken rice bowl' refers to someone who can no longer depend on the state to provide employment. It dates from the regime of Mao Zedong, when having an 'iron rice bowl' meant lifetime job security, and assumed complete loyalty to the Communist party, which controlled housing, marriage options, food rations and educational choices.

Negative racial stereotypes are embedded in the language of rice. During the Vietnam War, a child born to a Vietnamese woman and an African-American soldier was sometimes described as the 'colour of burnt rice'. In a poster from the same period, South Vietnam used the imagery of an abundant rice harvest combined with rows of marching soldiers, bayonets raised, as propaganda to support Vietnamese soldiers. They would be able to fight well and long, as long as there was rice to sustain them.

Vietnamese propaganda poster from the 1960s. The words, loosely translated, indicate that each grain is needed to have a full sack of rice, and, by analogy, that each soldier is needed to build a strong nation.

The Chinese-American author and educator Maxine Hong Kingston describes her grandfather's attitude toward girls in her book *The Woman Warrior* (1975) in terms of rice: 'The families are glad to be rid of them. Girls are maggots in the rice. It is more profitable to raise geese than daughters.' In the Philippines, *ampao* is the name of a puffed rice delicacy that, when used pejoratively, refers to someone with an empty head.

In *The Member of the Wedding* (1946), Carson McCullers describes the main character's love of rice:

> Now hopping-john was F. Jasmine's very favorite food. She had always warned them to wave a plate of rice and peas before her nose when she was in her coffin, to make certain there was no mistake; for if a breath of life was left in her, she would sit up and eat, but if she smelled the hopping-john and did not stir, then they could just nail down the coffin and be certain she was truly dead.

Rice in this Filipino song is a paean to hard physical work and drudgery:

Planting rice is never fun;
Bent from morn till set of sun;
Cannot stand and cannot sit;
Cannot rest for a little bit.

Amazingly, this song was sung in the American public school system in the Philippines after the Second World War, although its meaning seems to have been lost on those who chose it as an anthem, however well-intentioned they may have been.

Culture and Rice: The Special Case of Japan

The importance of rice to Japanese society has been studied extensively and will provide a window through which to view its symbolic value in detail.

The concept of group harmony, dependency and consensus are thought to spring from wet rice cultivation. Historically, families pooled their labour and skills. Wet rice cultivation is labour-intensive, involving skills that everyone must execute simultaneously. This includes planting seedlings, building canals and dykes and sharing water resources, all of which linked families in an area. Houses were clustered together and the whole community helped out and did the planting together, for each household. The same was true at harvest time. Communal decisions and group interests were emphasized over individual preference. Efforts to avoid friction between families who would be neighbours and workmates for generations were paramount. This historic commitment to group synchronization, a feature of the original culture of rice, continues today and shapes group consciousness. Even though a small number of people grow rice in Japan today, 124 million people still try to sustain group harmony daily, and in confined spaces.

The Japanese language provides clues to these concepts and values. The primacy of rice as a diet staple is echoed in the language. *Gohan* is both the word for 'cooked rice' and 'meal'. Adding prefixes to *gohan* gives us the words for breakfast (*asagohan*), lunch (*hirugohan*) and dinner (*bangohan*). These linguistic signals make it clear that thinking of a meal without rice is impossible.

Another indicator is the linguistic link to the early indigenous name of Japan, *mizuho no kuni* (the land of the water stalk plant or rice). Interestingly, the Japanese have identified the U.S. as *beikoku* (land of rice), thereby implying abundance.

Historically, rice has many links to Japanese culture. For example, the Emperor became a 'priest-king' early in Japanese history. His functions in Shintoism revolved around rice growing, and included making sake (rice wine) and *mochi* (rice cakes). Emperor Hirohito (1926–1989) tended a rice plot on the Imperial grounds in Tokyo, until he became seriously ill, and even then, he worried about the weather and the crops. Traditions are maintained as the current Emperor Akihito (*b.* 1933) blesses the rice crop. Many coronation ceremonies involving rice and rice products underscore links to the Emperor and to Shintoism.

Rice needed to be guarded, and represented security and prosperity, affirming its societal importance. *Sho*, a measure of rice, was used to determine wealth, in addition to being used as an instrument of trade, hard currency and as payment to samurai.

This small survey could be amplified by many examples from other aspects of Japanese life, including folklore, festivals,

Tanbo art – the famous Hokusai Great Wave 'painting' made from rice stalks, grass and other grains.

art and family rituals. All parts of the rice plant are fully utilized. Every year some 32 kg (70 lb) of stalks are recycled into each tatami mat, which are used for flooring in many Japanese homes. Bran is made into face scrubs. Rice paste was used in bookbinding, a resist-dye technique for fabrics and especially in silk for kimonos. Rice is so enmeshed in the culture that, while people in the U.S. refer to 'the man in the moon' or see a woman's face, the Japanese see 'a rabbit pounding rice cakes' (*mochi*), a reminder of a popular folktale.

Recipes

Recipes and cooking methods reflect a time and place in history. Most recipes were transmitted orally until 'receipts' began to be written down, first for the professional chefs of aristocratic households and the clergy (whether at the time of the Roman Apicius or the early twentieth-century Escoffier), and later for the middle classes. To date, pre-modern Arabic culture produced the greatest number of cookbooks of which examples still exist. The first recipes were prose texts, which assumed highly skilled culinary competencies.

I have listed first examples of two recipes – pilaf and gumbo – that are popular and have variants in many countries, followed by an idiosyncratic mix of recipes that have wide appeal across cultures.

Aruzz Mufalfal
—from Charles Perry's translation of a thirteenth-century recipe from a medieval Arabic cookery book called *Kitāb al Tabīkh*.

The way to make it is to take fat meat and cut it up medium. Melt fresh tail fat and throw away its cracklings, then throw the meat on it and stir until it is browned. Sprinkle a little salt and finely ground dry coriander on it. Then leave water to cover on it and boil it until it is done, and throw its scum away. Remove it from the pot after its liquid has dried up and it has started to stew, lest it be dry. Throw on as much dry coriander, cumin, cinnamon and finely ground mastic as it will bear, and likewise as much salt. When it is completely done, take it up from the pot, having been dried of moisture and fat. Sprinkle a little of those mentioned spices on it. Then take a measure of rice and three measures [and a half] of water. Melt fresh tail fat weighing one third as much as the meat. Throw the water in the pot. When it comes to [a boil], throw the melted fat on it. Throw mastic and sticks of cinnamon in it, then boil it until it comes to a full boil. Wash rice several times and colour it with saffron and throw it in the water; do not stir it. Then cover the pot awhile until the rice boils up and the water is boiling. Then open it and arrange that meat on top of the rice, and cover it with a cloth over the lid, and wrap it so that the air does not enter it. Then leave the pot until it grows quiet on a gentle fire for awhile, then take it up. Some people make it plain, not coloured with saffron.

Charles Perry's footnote indicates that 'aruzz' means rice, and 'mulfalfal' 'cooked to resemble peppercorns'; that is, as separate grains. He also mentions the possible influence of the Persian word '*pulau*' or 'pilaf'.

Pilaf with Golden Raisins and Pine Nuts

Pilaf can be made with bulgur and barley, but rice has pride of place. According to Claudia Roden in *The New Book of Middle Eastern Food* (2000), rice was introduced to Persia via India, and spread by Arabs southwest to Spain and as far south as Sicily. Called *roz* by Arabs, *pilav* by Turks, *chelow* by Iranians when plain and *polow* when other ingredients are added, pilaf can be served with stews, moulded, coloured red or yellow and otherwise prepared with vegetables, fruits, nuts, meat, fish, cream and milk. It can be served with all the other dishes or in sequence depending on where you are and with whom you are eating. Not surprisingly, there are many different kinds of long-grain rice used, each having its adherents.

My recipe for pilaf is a variation on Roden's classic Ottoman Empire Court recipe.

2 medium onions, chopped
15 ml (2 tbsp) canola oil
100 g (⅔ cup) pine nuts, toasted
400 g (2 cups) long-grain rice
675 ml (3 cups) chicken stock
1 tsp ground allspice
1 tsp cinnamon
1 tsp fenugreek seeds
salt and pepper
3 tbsp golden raisins
6 tbsp butter, cut into pieces
1 tbsp chopped dill

In a large pan, cook the onions in the oil until golden and soft. Add the pine nuts and rice and stir over a moderate heat until the rice grains and pine nuts are well coated with oil and starting to toast. Add the stock and stir in the allspice, cinnamon, fenugreek, salt, pepper and golden raisins. Bring to a boil, then simmer, covered, over a low heat for 20 minutes, or until the rice is tender. Stir in the butter and dill and serve hot.

Roden notes that for a Turkish variation you might add sautéed seasoned chicken livers and chopped dill to the hot rice.

Gumbo

Gumbo is a word, a recipe, a thick soupy stew, and a form of social commentary. The diverse ingredients that make up a gumbo could be said to represent a culinary dateline, where several strands of varying ethnic influences intersect, resulting in delicious and always interesting mixtures. Here are two versions, both from *The Carolina Rice Kitchen: The African Connection* (1992), with an Introduction to the annotated facsimile of *The Carolina Rice Cook Book*, compiled by Mrs Samuel G. Stoney in 1901.

New Orleans Gumbo

Take a turkey or fowl, cut it up with a piece of fresh beef, put them in a pot with a little lard, an onion and water sufficient to cook the meat. After they have become soft, add 100 oysters, with their liquor. Season to your taste, and just before taking up the soup, stir in, until it becomes mucilaginous, 2 spoonsful of pulverized sassafras leaves.

The phrase 'serve with rice' is missing from the text, but is assumed. Okra is also missing, but the sassafras presumably serves a similar thickening purpose.

Southern Gumbo

Slice 2 large onions, fry, have ready a good-sized chicken cut up; put in with the onions and fry brown. Have a quart of sliced okra and 4 large tomatoes; put all with the chicken in a stew pan and pour hot water over it. Let boil until thick; season with salt and red pepper pods. It must be dished and eaten with rice boiled.

Rice Puddings

Rice puddings exist in all rice cultures, both old and new. They vary in form from the simplest – soft and sweetened rice pudding – to *arroz con leche* made with condensed milk, or *riz a l'imperatrice*, a moulded creation of Escoffier's made in honour of the Empress Eugenie upon her marriage to Napoleon, which included vanilla custard, whipped cream and brandied fruit. In between are soft, firm, sliceable, spoonable, white, black and brown versions of rice pudding. Flavourings vary equally from vanilla and lemon zest, to cardamom, cashews, pistachios and saffron. Today rice puddings are made with dairy milk, soya milk, rice milk and coconut milk.

An American Colonial Rice Pudding
—from J. M. Sanderson, *The Complete Cook* (1846)

Rice Custard. – Take a cup of whole Carolina rice, and seven cups of milk; boil it, by placing the pan in water, which must never be allowed to go off the boil until it thickens; then sweeten it, and add an ounce of sweet almonds pounded.

Kheer

2 pt (1.1 litres) whole milk
2 tbsp long-grain rice, such as basmati
4 whole green cardamom pods, lightly crushed
10 unsalted pistachios
2 tbsp sugar

To decorate
vark (edible silver or gold leaf, available from specialist
cake shops or some Asian grocers),
chopped pistachios, optional

Pour the milk into a heavy-based pan and heat gently (you can pre-heat the milk in a jug in the microwave, then transfer the hot milk to the pan, to save time, if you prefer). Add the rice and cardamom pods to the milk.

Slowly bring to the boil, then lower the heat and simmer rapidly, stirring from time to time to prevent the rice from sticking to the bottom of the pan. Simmer, stirring occasionally, until the milk is reduced by about half; this may take as long as 1¼ hours. While the milk is simmering, roughly chop the pistachios.

When the milk has reduced by half or more, remove and discard the cardamom pods. Transfer the rice pudding to a bowl. Add the sugar and taste, adding more sugar if you want it sweeter. Add the chopped pistachios, stir well, and leave to cool.

Cover the bowl with cling film and cool in the fridge for at least four hours or overnight.

When ready to serve, spoon into individual serving bowls. Decorate with vark, if using.

Sprinkle a few more chopped pistachios on top, if liked.

Sticky Rice Pudding
(for those who are lactose intolerant)

675 ml (3 cups) vanilla-flavoured rice milk
200 g (1 cup) sticky rice
150 g (¾ cup) granulated sugar
1 tbsp fresh ginger, grated
grated zest of 1 lemon
¼ tsp salt
1 vanilla bean pod, cut and scraped (save the pod for the sugar
container or vodka bottle)
2 large eggs
1 egg yolk
1 tbsp candied lemon peel, finely chopped
2 tbsp dark rum

Combine 2 cups of rice milk, rice, ½ cup of the sugar, the ginger and zest in a medium saucepan. Bring to a boil. Immediately reduce the heat to a simmer and cover. Cook until most of the milk is absorbed into the rice, about 20–25 minutes. Remove from heat. Uncover and cool, about 30 minutes.

Whisk together the remaining milk, the remaining sugar, salt, vanilla bean paste, the eggs and yolk in a medium bowl. When well mixed, strain the mixture through a sieve into a large saucepan. Cook, over low – medium heat, stirring constantly until the mixture coats the back of a spoon, about 8 minutes. Remove from heat.

Add candied lemon peel, rum and the cooled rice mixture, stirring until all is well blended. The mixture should be somewhat loose.

Transfer the pudding to a serving bowl or divide evenly among 6 oiled (almond oil, or very good olive oil) custard cups, which can be flipped over to remove the rice puddings once they are set. Chill for several hours before unmoulding. Serve the pudding after it has been at room temperature for one hour.

Soft coconut or mango sorbet is a good accompaniment, along with a few drops of dense, aged balsamic vinegar sprinkled on top. *Serves 6*

Fried Rice

Fried rice is a preparation using leftover rice. Fried rice is probably far more common than any other way of using leftover cooked rice because it is fast and easy to prepare and uses up other leftovers in addition to the rice itself. Leftover rice has its own unique qualities and is prepared in ways that showcase them. All rice-consuming cultures have ways of using leftover rice that have become part of their culinary heritages.

Nasi Goreng

This recipe is the Indonesian and Malay variant of a Chinese way to make fried rice. I have adapted it from Michael Freeman, *Ricelands: The World of Southeast Asian Food* (London, 2008).

3 tbsp vegetable oil
3 cloves garlic, chopped
4 shallots, chopped
150 g (about 5 oz) raw prawns, peeled
150 g (about 5 oz) chicken cut into 5 cm (2 inches) pieces
1–2 tbsp light soy sauce
400 g (about 14 oz) leftover cold, cooked rice
4 eggs
2 spring onions, sliced to include some of the green stalks
3 medium-length fresh chillies, de-seeded and chopped

1 tbsp parsley, chopped
3 stalks coriander, leaves torn and chopped
pinch salt
pinch ground pepper

In a wok, heat the oil until almost smoking, then add the garlic and cook over a medium heat until it begins to turn golden-brown. Add the shallots and stir-fry until they begin to brown. Add the prawns, chicken and soy sauce and stir-fry until the prawns turn pink and the chicken loses its pinkness. Add the rice and stir continuously, mixing thoroughly with the prawns and chicken, for a few minutes, until hot. Cover and set aside. Fry the eggs in oil without breaking the yolks. Remove and set aside.

Scoop the rice out onto individual dishes, sprinkle the spring onions, chillies, parsley and coriander on top, add salt and pepper and finally place a fried egg on top of each.

Hoppin' John

Hoppin' John is an African-derived combination of rice and beans/pigeon peas whose history spans hundreds if not thousands of years, even though the recipe here is in modern format, and is made with modern rice. African and Asian rice, and all kinds of beans, are combined to create national dishes that have become part of the culinary profiles of different countries. Scholars of African and African-American foodways, including Karen Hess, Jessica Harris and James McWilliams, have speculated upon the origins of the term 'hoppin' John'. There is no consensus. *Arroz con frijoles* is the Latin version of rice and beans or hoppin' John, found throughout the Caribbean, Mexico and South America.

This recipe is adapted from Jessica Harris, *The Welcome Table: African American Heritage Cooking* (New York, 1995).

1 pound (450 g) dried black-eyed peas (cowpeas)
½ pound (225 g) salt pork
1 quart (950 ml) water

1 sprig fresh thyme
salt and freshly ground black pepper, to taste
1 ½ cups (150 g) raw long-grain rice
3 cups (675 ml) hot water

Pick over the black-eyed peas to remove dirt and stones. Soak them in water to cover at least 4 hours or overnight. Fry the salt pork in a large heavy casserole to render the fat. When the salt pork is crisp, add the black-eyed peas and the quart of water, the thyme, salt and pepper, cover, and cook over low heat for 40 minutes. Adjust the seasonings and continue to cook until the peas are tender. Add the rice, cover with the 3 cups hot water, and simmer over low heat until all of the liquid has been absorbed and the rice is tender. Serve hot.

On New Year's Day, in some families, a dime is placed in the hoppin' John to ensure special good luck throughout the year for the person who gets it.

Oysters and Rice: A Gullah Recipe

This recipe is from the Low Country: the coastal Sea Islands off the coast of Georgia (in the U.S.) where the African-American inhabitants are known as 'Gullahs', the 'people who eat rice'. It is adapted from Sallie Ann Robinson and Gregory Wrenn Smith, *Gullah Home Cooking the Daufuskie Way* (2003).

4 strips bacon
1 tablespoon cooking oil
1 large onion, chopped
1 medium-green bell pepper, chopped
2 tablespoons flour
3 cups (675 ml) warm water
salt and black pepper to taste
2 cups (400 g) uncooked rice
1 quart (1 kg) shucked oysters, drained

Fry the bacon until crisp in a medium pot. Remove the bacon, leaving the grease in the pot. Add the oil, onion and bell pepper, and stir-fry until the onion is clear. Remove the onion and bell pepper, leaving the oil and grease. Brown the flour in the oil and grease, and then return the bacon, onion and bell pepper to the pot. Add the water, season to taste with salt and pepper, bring to a boil, lower the heat, and simmer 15 minutes, stirring often, to form a thin gravy. Rinse and strain the rice several times and rinse the oysters, then add both to the pot. Combine thoroughly, cover, and simmer, stirring occasionally, 30 to 45 minutes. Serve as a meal, with vegetable side dishes.

Rice Waffles
—adapted from Fannie Merritt Farmer, *The Boston Cooking School Cook Book* (1896)

1¾ cups (600 g) flour
4 teaspoons baking powder
⅔ cup (90 g) cold cooked rice
¼ teaspoon salt
1½ cups (340 ml) milk
1 tablespoon melted butter
2 tablespoons sugar
1 egg

Mix and sift dry ingredients; work in rice with tips of fingers; add milk, yolk of egg well beaten, butter, and white of egg beaten stiff. Cook same as Waffles.

Rice à la Roast

The following recipe is adapted from a 1971 booklet published by the Rice Council of America in Houston, Texas. *Man-pleasing Recipes* begins with the phrase 'No man likes the same thing every night!' Rice recipes are given for breakfast, lunch and dinner. Adding zest to your family meals is the stated goal. 'Recipes for the vegetable part of the plate or for the elegant dinner. Tasty – try them!'

1 cup (125 g) chopped green onions, with tops
½ cup (60 g) chopped green pepper
2 tablespoons butter or margarine
3 cups (400 g) hot cooked rice, cooked in beef broth
3 tablespoons chopped pimiento
salt and pepper

Sauté onions and green pepper in butter until tender crisp. Add rice and pimiento. Toss lightly. Adjust seasonings to taste. Serve with your favourite roast.
Serves 6

Steamed Rice II
—adapted from Gloria Bley Miller, *The Thousand Recipe Chinese Cookbook* (New York, 1970)

Wash rice thoroughly. Place in a pan with plenty of water. Boil for 5 minutes, stirring a few times. Drain.

Place the rice in a bamboo steamer lined with cheesecloth. Pierce the rice several times with chopsticks or fork, making small holes to let the steam pass through.

Cover the pan and steam over a medium heat for 20 minutes.

Miller notes that the liquid drained in step 2 can be mixed with sugar and served separately as a thin *congee*.

Rosematta Rice
—adapted from Jeffrey Alford and Naomi Duguid, *Seductions of Rice* (New York, 2003)

This unusual parboiled red rice from South India is only partially milled: part of the reddish bran layer is left intact. Despite being parboiled, the rice is rinsed to remove debris and scum that forms when first cooking. It has an *umami* or meaty aroma and the grains easily stay separated from each other.

2 cups (400 g) rice
3 cups (675 ml) water (2¼ cups or 500 ml if using a rice cooker)

Wash the rice thoroughly under running water. The water will run reddish brown at first. Place in a sieve to drain. Pick through the rice and discard any hard kernels or other irregularities. Place in a heavy medium pot or in a rice cooker and add the water. If using a pot, bring to a vigorous boil, stir briefly, and boil uncovered for 3 to 4 minutes. Stir again, cover, and lower the heat to medium-low. Simmer for 5 minutes, then reduce the heat to very low and cook, still covered, for another 12 to 15 minutes. Let stand for another 10 to 15 minutes, without lifting the lid, to steam, then stir gently with a wooden paddle. The rice should be firm, bouncy even, and cooked through.

If using a rice cooker, turn on, cover and let cook. When the cooker turns off, let stand, covered for 10 to 15 minutes, before stirring.

Chicken Congee

Breakfast for many, comfort food for all: *congee* is often eaten with salty pickles, soy sauce, salted peanuts, radishes, pickled ginger, preserved greens, sausage, salted fish and any other leftovers that are handy. This recipe is adapted from Hsiang Ju Lin and Tsuifeng Lin, *Chinese Gastronomy* (New York, 1977).

100 g (½ cup) river rice (short-grain or other high-starch rice)
6 cups (1.35 litres) chicken stock
1 chicken breast
½ level teaspoon salt
2 tablespoons water

Wash rice. Bring it to the boil in chicken stock; then reduce heat to very low and simmer for 2 hours. Meanwhile, skin and bone the chicken breast and slice it with the grain. Flatten the slices with a few whacks of the side of the cleaver. Add salt and water. When the *congee* is ready to serve, turn off the heat. Stir the chicken slices, then stir them into the *congee* and let it stand for 3 to 4 minutes. Serve in bowls.

Pulot Hitam (Malaysian Black Rice Porridge)
—adapted from Charmaine Solomon, *Encyclopedia of Asian Food*
(Boston, 1998)

220 g (1 cup) black glutinous rice
1.5 litres (3 pt) water
60 g (2 oz) palm sugar
2 tablespoons granulated sugar
2 strips pandan leaf
6 dried longans
250 ml (8 fl oz) coconut cream
¼ teaspoon salt

Wash rice in several changes of water and drain. Put into a heavy saucepan with the measured water and bring to the boil. Cover and simmer for 30–40 minutes, stirring occasionally to make sure the rice doesn't stick to the bottom of the pan. Add palm sugar and granulated sugar, pandan leaf and dried longans. (If the longans are still in their shells, discard the shells.) If the porridge becomes too thick, add more hot water. Continue cooking until the rice grains have become very soft. Serve warm, with coconut cream to which the salt has been added.
Serves 6

Brown Rice Horchata
—adapted from www.massaorganics.com

½ cup (100 g) sugar
1 bag (7 oz, 350 g) unsweetened coconut flakes (use less sugar
if you use sweetened coconut flakes)
¾ cup (150 g) brown rice, soaked overnight and drained
1 cup (135 g) blanched almonds, toasted
1 cinnamon stick
¼ cup (55 ml) vanilla rice milk

Put sugar and 5 tablespoons water into a small saucepan, cover
and boil over medium heat, swirling the pan occasionally, until the
sugar dissolves, 4 to 5 minutes. Transfer to a bowl and allow the
syrup to cool.

Put the coconut and 1½ cups water into a blender and purée
until smooth. Strain through a fine sieve into a bowl, pressing on
solids with a rubber spatula to extract as much coconut milk as
possible, and set aside.

Put the rice, almonds, cinnamon and 2 cups water into clean
blender and purée until smooth. Strain mixture through a cheese-
cloth-lined sieve into a bowl, pressing on solids to extract as much
liquid as possible, and then return strained mixture to a clean blender.
Add ¾ cup of the coconut milk, the syrup, rice milk and 2 cups ice
cubes to blender and purée until ice is well chopped and drink is
frothy. Divide between 2 to 4 glasses and serve immediately.
Serves 2–4

Pearly Meat Balls

—adapted from Hsiang Ju Lin and Tsuifeng Lin, *Chinese Gastronomy*
(New York, 1977)

2½ oz (6 level tablespoons) glutinous rice
1 level teaspoon salt
¼ lb (100 g) fat pork, minced (ground)
¼ lb (100 g) lean pork, minced (ground)
1½ teaspoons wine
½ level teaspoon sugar
2 teaspoons light soy sauce
1 level tablespoon cornflour (cornstarch)
½ level teaspoon MSG
oil
5 tablespoons soy sauce
3 tablespoons vinegar

Put the rice in a 2-pint measuring cup (4-cup Pyrex bowl), and fill it to the 24 fluid oz (3 cup) mark with water. Let stand for 45 minutes, then drain it. Mix rice with salt.

In a separate bowl, mix together the pork, wine, sugar, soy sauce, cornflour, MSG and 1 tablespoon water. Blend the meat thoroughly with seasoning and shape it into 1-inch balls. Roll the balls in the glutinous rice and place them on an oiled plate of dish. Cover it closely and steam it for 30 minutes. Serve with soy sauce and vinegar, mixed together in a separate dish.

Epasol (Sweet Rice Flour Cakes)
—adapted from Reynaldo Alejandro, *The Philippine Cookbook*
(New York, 1985)

This Philippine recipe comes with the admonition that Philippine etiquette involves serving all dishes or courses at once, including sweet and savoury dishes together. This is not necessarily a dessert.

4 cups (560 g) sweet rice flour
1 ½ cups (150 g) sugar
2 cans coconut milk
½ tsp salt

Toast the sweet rice flour on a cookie sheet. Bring sugar, coconut milk and salt to a boil. Add 3 cups toasted sweet rice flour. Mix well and cook until thick, stirring constantly. Remove from heat and transfer to board well sprinkled with some of the reserved sweet rice flour. With a rolling pin, flatten to about ¼ inch and cut into diamonds. Roll in remaining rice flour.
Makes 15 to 20 cakes

Rice Noodles

Rice noodles can be fresh or dried, long or short, thin or thick, and may even come in pre-cooked broad sheets that can be cut or shaped as you wish. China and Thailand are the largest exporters of rice noodles. Some are made with rice flour, others with sticky rice flour, and yet others with different flours (such as tapioca or cornstarch) for springiness and texture.

Fresh rice sheets can be sliced or stuffed, and must be eaten before they dry out. Dried rice noodles, also called rice sticks, should be soaked in room-temperature water for 10 to 20 minutes to soften, and then added to the cooking process, otherwise they will become mushy. To remove excess starch, so as to keep the broth clear if you are making soup, rice noodles can be briefly boiled after soaking.

Singapore Noodles

—adapted from Corinne Trang, *Noodles Every Day: Delicious Asian Recipes from Ramen to Rice Sticks* (San Francisco, 2009)

This recipe is popular in Chinese restaurants in the u.s., and uses left-over Cantonese roast pork and curry powder, which showcases Indian influence in Singapore.

8 oz (225 g) dried rice vermicelli, soaked in water until pliable
24 small tiger shrimp, heads removed, peeled and deveined
3 tbsp vegetable oil
1 small onion, cut into small wedges
½ cup (75 g) fresh shelled peas, or thawed frozen peas
2 tsp curry powder (Indian)
6 oz (175 g) Cantonese roast pork
1 ½ tbsp fish sauce
Kosher salt and freshly ground pepper
6 sprigs coriander, trimmed

Cook the noodles in a pot of boiling water until tender, about 10 seconds. Transfer them to a bowl. In same water cook the shrimps, about 1 minute.

Heat 1 tablespoon of oil in a skillet or wok, and stir-fry onion until golden, about 3–4 minutes. Add other 2 tablespoons oil, the noodles and peas. Sprinkle curry powder on top. Toss well, making sure all noodles become yellow. Add pork, shrimp, fish sauce and heat thoroughly, stir frying all the while, about 5 minutes. Adjust seasoning with salt and pepper, and serve with coriander.
Serves 6

Select Bibliography

Achaya, K. T., *Historical Dictionary of Indian Food* (Oxford, 2001)

Al-Baghdadi, Mohammad Ibn Al-Hasah, *A Baghdad Cookery Book* (Blackawton, Totnes, Devon, 2006)

Alcock, Joan P., *Food in the Ancient World* (London, 2006)

Anderson, E. N., *The Food of China* (New Haven, CT, 1990)

Balfour, Edward, *The Cyclopaedia of India and of Eastern and Southern Asia: Commercial, Industrial and Scientific Products of the Mineral, Animal and Vegetable Kingdoms, Useful Arts and Manufacture* (London, 1885)

Barnes, Cynthia, 'The Art of Rice', *Humanities*, 24 (September–October 2003), www.neh.gov

Beeton, Isabella Mary, ed., *Mrs Beeton's Book of Household Management* (London, 1861)

Boesch, Mark J., *The World of Rice: Its History, Geography and Science* (New York, 1967)

Bray, Francesca, *The Rice Economies: Technology and Development in Asian Societies* (Berkeley, CA, 1994)

Burton, David, *The Raj at Table: A Culinary History of the British in India* (London, 1993)

Carney, Judith, 'The African Antecedents of Uncle Ben in U.S. Rice History', *Journal of Historical Geography*, 29 (1 January 2003), pp. 1–21

—, 'African Rice in the Columbian Exchange', *Journal of African History*, XLII/3 (2001), pp. 377–96

—, 'From Hands to Tutors: African Expertise in the South

Carolina Rice Economy', *Agricultural History*, 67
(Summer 1993), pp. 1–30

—, '"With Grains in Her Hair": Rice in Colonial Brazil',
Slavery and Abolition, XXV/1 (2004), pp. 1–27

Coclanis, Peter A., 'The Poetics of American Agriculture: The
United States Rice Industry in International Perspective',
Agricultural History, 69 (Spring 1995), pp. 140–62

—, *The Shadow of a Dream: Economic Life and Death in the South
Carolina Low Country, 1670–1920* (New York, 1989)

—, 'Southeast Asia's Incorporation into the World Rice Market:
A Revisionist View', *Journal of Southeast Asian Studies*, XXIV/2
(1993), pp. 251–67

—, 'Breaking New Ground: From the History of Agriculture
to the History of Food Systems', *Historical Methods*, 38
(Winter 2005), pp. 5–15

Cole, Arthur Harrison, *Wholesale Commodity Prices in the United
States, 1700–1861* (Cambridge, MA, 1938)

Collingham, Lizzie, *Curry: A Tale of Cooks and Conquerors*
(Oxford and New York, 2006)

Corson, Trevor, *The Story of Sushi: An Unlikely Saga of Raw
Fish and Rice* (New York, 2008)

Davidson, Alan, *The Oxford Companion to Food*, 2nd edn
(New York, 2006)

Davis, Lucille, *Court Dishes of China: The Cuisines of the Ch'ing
Dynasty* (Rutland, VT, and Tokyo, 1966)

Dethloff, Henry C., *A History of the American Rice Industry*,
1685–1985 (College Station, TX, 1988)

Ewing, J. C., *Creole Mammy Rice Recipes* (Crowley, LA, 1921)

Fragner, Bert, From the Caucasus to the Roof of the World: A
Culinary Adventure', in Sami Zubaida and Richard Tapper,
eds, *Culinary Cultures of the Middle East* (London, 1994)

Freeman, Michael, *Ricelands: The World of South-East Asian Food*
(London, 2008)

Grist, D. H., *Rice*, 6th edn (New York, 1986)

Hall, Gwendolyn Midlo, *Africans in Colonial Louisiana: The
Development of Afro-Creole Culture in the Eighteenth Century*
(Baton Rouge, LA, 1992)

Hansen, Eric, 'The Nonya Cuisine of Malaysia: Fragrant Feasts
    Where the Trade Winds Meet', *Saudi Aramco World*, 54
    (September–October 2003), pp. 32–9
Harris, Jessica, *Beyond Gumbo: Creole Fusion Food from the Atlantic
    Rim* (New York, 2003)
—, *Iron Pots and Wooden Spoons: Africa's Gifts to New World Cooking*
    (New York, 1989)
Hess, Karen, *The Carolina Rice Kitchen: The African Connection*
    (Columbia, SC, 1992)
Higham, Charles, and Tracey L.-D Lu, 'The Origins and
    Dispersal of Rice Cultivation', *Antiquity*, 72 (December
    1998), pp. 867–77
Huggan, Robert D., 'Co-Evolution of Rice and Humans',
    GeoJournal, 35 (1995), pp. 262–5
Kingston, Maxine Hong, *The Woman Warriors: Memoirs
    of a Girlhood Among Ghosts* (New York, 1975)
Kumar, Tuk-Tuk, *History of Rice in India: Mythology, Culture
    and Agriculture* (New Delhi, 1988)
Latham, A.J.H., *Rice: The Primary Commodity* (London and
    New York, 1998)
McWilliams, James E., *A Revolution in Eating: How the Quest for
    Food Shaped America* (New York, 2005)
Mancall, Peter C., Joshua L. Rosenbloom and Thomas Weiss,
    'Slave Prices and the Economy of the Lower South,
    1722–1809', conference paper, January 2000, at www.eh.net.
Medina, F. Xavier, *Food Culture in Spain* (Westport, CT, 2005)
Mintz, Sidney W., 'Asia's Contributions to World Cuisine',
    in Sidney C. H. Cheung and Tan Chee-Beng, eds,
    Food and Foodways in Asia (Abingdon, 2007), pp. 201–10
Ohnuki-Tierney, Emiko, 'Rice as Self: Japanese Identities
    Through Time', *Education About Asia*, 9 (Winter 2004),
    pp. 4–9
Owen, Sri, *The Rice Book* (London, 1993)
Piper, Jacqueline M., *Rice in South-East Asia: Cultures
    and Landscapes* (New York, 1994)
Robinson, Sallie Ann, with Gregory Wrenn Smith, *Gullah Home
    Cooking the Daufuskie Way: Smokin' Joe Butter Beans, O' 'Fuskie*

Fried Rice, Sticky-Bush Blackberry Dumpling, and Other Sea Island Favorites (Chapel Hill, NC, 2003)

Roden, Claudia, *Arabesque. A Taste of Morocco, Turkey, and Lebanon* (New York, 2006)

—, *The Food of Spain* (New York, 2011).

—, *The New Book of Middle Eastern Food*, revd edn (New York, 2000)

Rodinson, Maxime, A. J. Arberry and Charles Perry, *Medieval Arab Cookery: Essays and Translations* (Blackawton, Totnes, Devon, 2001)

Sen, Colleen Taylor, *Curry: A Global History* (London, 2009)

Simmons, Marie, *The Amazing World of Rice: With 150 Recipes for Pilafs, Paellas, Puddings, and More* (New York, 2002)

Smith, Andrew, ed., *The Oxford Encylopedia of Food and Drink in America* (Oxford, 2004)

Smith, C. Wayne, and Robert Henry Dilday, eds, *Rice: Origins, History, Technology, and Production* (Hoboken, NJ, 2003)

Sokolov, Raymond, 'A Matter of Taste: A Two-Faced Grain', *Natural History*, 102 (January 1993), pp. 68–70

Walker, Harlan, *Staple Foods: Proceedings of the Oxford Symposium on Food and Cookery* (Blackawton, Totnes, Devon, 1990)

West, Jean M., 'Rice and Slavery: A Fatal Gold Seedc', www.slaveryinamerica.org, accessed 22 April 2011

Wright, Clifford, *A Mediterranean Feast: The Story of the Birth of the Celebrated Cuisines of the Mediterranean, from the Merchants of Venice to the Barbary Corsairs* (New York, 1999)

Yin-Fei Lo, Eileen, *The Chinese Kitchen: Recipes, Techniques, History, and Memories from America's Leading Authority on Chinese Cooking* (New York, 1999)

Zafaralla, P. B., *Rice in the Seven Arts* (Laguna, Philippines, 2004)

Zaouali, Lilia, M. B. DeBevoise and Charles Perry, *Medieval Cuisine of the Islamic World: A Concise History with 174 Recipes* (Berkeley, CA, 2009)

Zubaida, Sami, and Richard Tapper, eds, *A Taste of Thyme: Culinary Cultures of the Middle East* (London and New York, 2000)

Websites and Associations

Rice Production and Research

Asia Rice
http://asiarice.org

Western Farm Press
http://westernfarmpress.com

American Association of Cereal Chemists
www.aaccnet.org

Africa Rice
www.africarice.org

Asia Society
www.asiasociety.org

The Chartered Institute of Architectural Technologists
www.ciat.cgiar.org

Economic Research Service, USDA
www.ers.usda.gov

Euromonitor
www.euromonitor.com

Food and Agriculture Organization
www.fao.gov

Food Timeline
www.foodtimeline.org

Grain
www.grain.org

International Rice Research Institute
www.irri.org

Lotus Foods
www.lotusfoods.com

Riceweb
www.riceweb.org

U.S. Rice Producers
www.usriceproducers.com

Recipes

Flavor and Fortune
www.flavorandfortune.com

Clifford A. Wright
www.cliffordawright.com

Mex Connect
www.mexconnect.com

On the Table
www.onthetable.us

Sri Owen
www.sriowen.com

Acknowledgements

I would like to thank the following individuals for their help while I researched *Rice: A Global History*: Jay Barksdale, Phil Bruno, Robert Carmack, Amy Cole, Dori Erlich, Barry Estabrook, Suzanne Fass, Alex Garcia, Joan Giurdanella, Jenny Huston, J. J. Jacobson, Rachel Laudan, Monique Lignon, Charlotte Lindberg, Mai Ling, Jan Longone, Vanessa Lucin, Danielle Marton, Gary Marton, Simone Marton, Joanna McNamara, Hung Nguyen, Margaret Happel Perry, Morrison Polkinghorne, Judy Rusignolo, Marie Simmons, Andy Smith, Jane Stanicki, Rick Stein, Gary Taubes, Laura Weiss, David Wexler, Stacia Wilkie, Sarah Wormer and especially Ed Smith.

I would also like to thank the New York Public Library, the Clements Library in Ann Arbor, Michigan, and libraries in cities everywhere, without which our lives would be inestimably poorer. Databases, while invaluable, are not enough.

While I received much help from many people, any errors are mine.

Photo Acknowledgements

The author and publishers wish to express their thanks to the below sources of illustrative material and/or permission to reproduce it. Some locations of artworks are also given below.

Courtesy http://allhindugods.blogspot.com/2013/01/pongal-kolam.html: p. 98; Asian Art Museum, Toronto: p. 97; photos by the author: pp. 8, 20 (foot), 32, 34, 58; photo bdspn/iStockphoto: p. 66; from 'Mrs Beeton', *The Book of Household Management . . . by Isabella Mary Beeton* (London, 1861): p. 50; bonchan/iStockphoto: p. 23; bopav/iStockphoto: p. 93; British Library, London (photos © The British Library Board): pp. 42, 99; photos © The Trustees of the British Museum, London: pp. 50, 64; Brooklyn Museum, New York (licensed under a Creative Commons-BY License): p. 46; photos Amy Cole: pp. 20 (top), 89; Amy Cole, after a map from Asia Society of New York: p. 37; graytown/iStockphoto: p. 56; photo Hargrett Rare Book and Manuscript Library/University of Georgia Libraries: p. 51; harikarn/iStockphoto: p. 81; photo ildi/iStockphoto: p. 60; photo Jastrow: p. 95; Library of Congress, Washington, DC: pp. 53, 77; lilly3/iStockphoto: p. 62; MickyWiswedel/iStockphoto: p. 15; Musée du Louvre, Paris: p. 95; photo nitram76/iStockphoto: p. 44; © Rachel Park from art@pota-laworld.com: p. 31; piotr_malczyk/iStockphoto: p. 16; Quaker Puffed Rice Machine – image courtesy of the Anderson Center: p. 76; photo quintanilla (© CanStockphoto Inc., 2013): p. 43; robyn-mac/iStockphoto: p. 78; photo subinpumsom/iStockphoto: p. 12;

Index

italic numbers refer to illustrations; **bold** to recipes

Afghanistan 39
Africa 9, 14, 41, 63
    African rice 45–6 , 61, 62
aghonibora 27
agriculture, rice 19, 26–7
    upland rice *see* dry cultivation
    vertical 14
    wet rice 14
Akihito, emperor of Japan 109
Alexander the Great 41
Anson Mills 53
Appert 73
Arkansas 56–7
Armstrong, Louis 106
aromatic rice 21
arroz con pollo 59
aruzz mufalfal **113–14**
arsenic 14–15
Asian rice (Oryza sativa) 19

Baghdad 41
Bangladesh 14, 21
Basmati 21, 22, 24, 82
Bayless, Rick 60
Beeton, Mrs, *Book of Household Management* 48–9, *50*

bhel puri 40
biryani 37, 65
Borlaug, Norman 26
Brazil 18, 61–3
    feijoada complete 61
Britain
    and colonialism 10
    and India 63–7
brown rice 15–16, *16*, 19
Buddhism 36
Budweiser beer 11

California
    rice ('Calrose') 57
    Sacramento 7–8, 57
California roll 9–10, 86
Cantonese immigrants 8
Carolina Golde *see* South Carolina
Central Rice Research Institute, India 27
cereal 13, 29, 63
Champa rice 33
Charleston, South Carolina 9, 47, 51, 53
China 7, 8, 14, 18, 30, 35

and Spanish colonies 58–9
Chinese restaurants 80
Civil War, u.s. (1861–5) 52
climate change 27
congee 7, 16, 32
  chicken congee **124–5**
consumption, rice 18
cooking rice
  boiling / steaming 31
  in fat 60
  parboiling 77
  rice cooker 89, *90*
Cream of Rice 32
Cuba 58–9
Cuu Long Delta Rice Research
  Institute, Vietnam 27

DeDomenico, Vince 78
de Soto, Hernándo 55
deep-water rice 14
dosa 10
dry cultivation 14
Dutch East India Company 67

Egypt 42

farming, rice
  nongshi 33
  paddy workers *33*
festivals 96–104
flaked rice 40
floodplain rice 27
food preservation 73–4
fried rice 9, **119**
  Nasi Goreng **119**
Fujian 9

Gair, Robert 73
Galen

and Anthimus 41–2
genetically engineered (GE) rice 27
Glasse, Hannah, *The Art of
  Cookery* 48
glutinous rice 22–3, 31
Grand Canal, China 35
Great Wall of China 31
Green Revolution 26
Guangzhou, China
gumbo 54, *55*, **115–16**

Han dynasty 39
Hanoi theatre 92
Himalayas 30
Hirohito, emperor of Japan 109
hoppin' John 9, 48, 54, *56*, **120–21**
horchata 10, *60*, 61, **126**
human migration *see* immigration
Huzenlaub, Eric 77

ikan briani 37, **37**
immigration 7, 9, 15, 70–71
India 26
  and Britain 63–7
  Indian cooking 39
  Indian rice 21
  Raj era 63
Indica rice 21, 40
Indonesia 67–8
International Rice Research
  Institute (IRRI), Philippines
  18, 26, 27
Iran 14, 82, 83, 114
irrigated rice 14, 27, 29, 39, 42,
  43, 45, 47, 56, 94
Islam 36, 41–3
Italy 41, 42, 55
  see also risotto

Japan 79–80
    culture and rice 108–10
    sushi 85–7, *85*
Japonica rice 21
Jasmine rice *see* aromatic rice
Javanica rice 36, 40
Jefferson, Thomas 47
jhal-muri 10
Johnstone, McKewn 52

kedgeree 67
Kingston, Maxine Hong,
    The Woman Warrior 107
Kogi BBQ truck 84
Koldihwa, India 30
Korea 26, 102
    Choson dynasty 102
    rice candy *101*
    Sorori 30

Laos
laser-levelling 26–7
Linnaeus, Carl 45
long-grain rice
Los Angeles
Louisiana 54–7
    and Germans 55
    Cajun 54
    Creole 54; *see also* Mammy
Rice
    Western Railroad 56
lowland rice
Lucas, Jonathan 52

McCullers, Carson, *The Member
    of the Wedding* 107
Malaysia 36–7
    cookery 37
    lakhsha 38–9

Malacca 36, *37*
    rice pudding *38*
Mammy Rice 56
Maritime Silk Road 35
mathematics, study of 94
Mexico 59
Minute Rice 79

NERICA 46
New Year's Day 9, 54, 100, 102,
    121
New York 9, 10, 52, 59, 71, 81
Nobel Peace Prize *see* Borlaug,
    Norman

Owen, Sri 38
Oysters and Rice **121–2**

paella 24, 82
Pakistan 21
partially milled rice 13
Pearly Meat Balls **127**
Persia 25, 39, 41
pestle and mortar 31, 40, 45
pilaf 39, 65, **82–3**
    with currants and pine nuts
    114–15
Peru 58–9
Philippines 23, 30, 40, 71, 96, 108
Polo, Marco 34
Pongal rice festival 98–9
Porras, Nadia Garcia 58
porridge 31
    chou 34
Portugal 61–3
processed rice products 69–71
puddling 29
puffed rice 40, *66*
    cereal *77*

pulut hitam 38, **125**
puso 15

Qianlong, emperor of China 34
Quaker puffed rice *76*

religion and origin myths 93–6
    Buddha 105
    Dewi Sri 96–7, *97*
    Hinduism 36
    Humidhid 96
    Inari, Japanese rice god 96
    Krishna 105
    Mae Posop, Thai rice
      goddess 92
    Ponniamman 95
    rice shrines 92, *93*
Rice à la Roast **122–3**
rice balls 22, *24*
rice bran oil 32
rice cakes 79
    epasol **128**
rice flour 13
Rice Krispies 76
rice noodles *32*, **128–9**
rice paddy
    irrigation 27
rice panicle 30, *30*
rice paper 31–2, *81*
rice puddings
    Kheer **117**
    Sticky Rice Pudding **118**
rice stalks 32
rice waffles **122**
rice-husking machine *20*
Rice Research and Extension
    Center Institute, Arkansas 27
rijsttafel 67–8

risotto 81, **81–2**
rosematta rice **123–4**
Rutledge, Edward 47
Rutledge, Sarah, *The Carolina
    Housewife* 48

St Louis World's Fair 76
sake 87–8, *88*
San Francisco, California 78
Sanderson, J. M., *The Complete
    Cook* 49
shifting cultivation 29
Silk Road 35
Singapore
slaves 46, 47–50, *51*
    in Brazil 61–2
Smith, Eliza, *The Compleat
    Housewife* 48
soccarat 24
Song Dynasty 33
South Carolina 47, 48, 51
Southern Rice Growers
    Association 56
Southwest Silk Road 35
Spain 58–9
    norias 43, *43*
    see also Louisiana
Spirit Cave, Thailand 30
Sri Lanka
steamed rice **123**
sticky rice *12*, 16, 21, 22, 23
    Thai *25*
    street food 83–4
sushi 85–7, *85*
sweet rice (*mochi*) 23

tahdig 16, 26, 83
Taiwan 9, 40

tamales *62*
Thailand 22, 23, 30, 72, 74, 85
Tisnawati 94
trade, in rice 36, 47
Turkey 8, 41

Umeya Rice Cake Company 79
Uncle Ben's 21, 77
urbanization 35, 69
    see also processed rice products
U.S. Department of Agriculture
    (USDA) 22
Uzbekistan 8
Veeraswamy's 65
Vietnam 23, 84
Vietnam War 106

West Indies 9, 47, 51, 62
wedding ceremonies 104
wetland rice *see* agriculture
white rice 16, *17*, 19
Woodward, Dr Henry 47

Yangtzi River Valley, China 30
Yunnan province, China 22, 100